GLOBAL FASHION LOCAL TRADITION

On the Globalisation of Fashion

D1328201

JAN BRAND Editor

JOSÉ TEUNISSEN Editor

ANNE VAN DER ZWAAG Author

GOSEWIJN VAN BEEK Author

SUMATI NAGRATH Author

SANDRA NIESSEN Author

SUSANNAH FRANKEL Author

TED POLHEMUS Author

TERRA

INTRODUCTION

The GLOBAL FASHION/LOCAL TRADITION project began as a programme of research and activities organised by the ArtEZ Fashion Professorship and the dAcapo-ArtEZ General Studies department at ArtEZ Institute of the Arts. The results of the workshops and the research were presented on 31 January 2005 during a symposium under the same name in the Arnhem Municipal Theatre. They also served as the basis for the exhibition held at the Centraal Museum and for this book. Every year the ArtEZ Fashion Professorship works on a topical theme that broaches an essential aspect of contemporary fashion, thus demonstrating that fashion is a mirror of its time in which important social and cultural developments can be recognised. By placing fashion in a theoretical and social context, underlying layers of meaning are revealed and opened for discussion.

For us, GLOBAL FASHION/LOCAL TRADITION was a rich and challenging theme that allowed us to point out a number of important changes in contemporary fashion and to chart the cultural consequences . The Internet and the enormous rise in the Fashion Week phenomenon on every continent means that fashion is no longer something strictly regulated by the West. Since the eighties, the most talked-about fashion designers have been Japanese, Africans and Turks who are appreciated because of the non-Western aesthetic they bring to the Paris catwalks. As a result, designers all over the world during the past decade have been reflecting intensely on their origins and their original culture. Crafts-manship, clothing traditions and idiosyncratic aesthetic notions are applied in recognisable ways and interwoven with international fashion trends.

The exhibition and book depict and describe this current development in fashion.

We would like to thank all those who worked on this project for their efforts and professional commitment, as well as the subsidisers and sponsors for their financial contributions and the trust they placed in us.

JOSÉ TEUNISSEN
Curator of Fashion and Costumes Centraal Museum Utrecht
Professor of Fashion, ArtEZ Institute of the Arts

JAN BRAND
Head of dAcapo-ArtEZ
General Studies department at ArtEZ Institute of the Arts

CONTENTS

detail RAZU MIKHINA, a/w 2003/2004

detail JOHN GALLIANO, a/w 2004/2005

detail SITS

José Teunissen

GLOBAL FASHION LOCAL TRADITION

On the globalisation of fashion

Society has become globalised, the effects of which are visible everywhere. McDonald's, Pizza Hut and Levi's stores are cropping up in every city and town, with the result that shopping streets the world over are becoming more and more uniform. The latest fashion can be seen worldwide on television, in magazines and in particular via the Internet. On style.com, Vogue's website, complete reportages of all the designs are shown a day after the shows. H&M now manages to have knock-offs hanging in their shops six weeks after the shows are over. In this they're faster than the designers themselves, who sell their designs to shops first and only then go into production. Six months after the official presentation they deliver their designs, the moment the actual summer or winter season begins. The paradox is that today the mass product – the copy – has overtaken the original design, as it were. Fashion spreads faster than the product itself.

FASHION AND COMMUNICATION

Fashion has always been international. Even in the eighteenth century small dolls dressed in the latest styles were circulating among the French and English royal houses, where the new fashions were initiated. With the advent of magazines and newspapers in the nineteenth century, specialised publications reporting the latest fashion news soon appeared, and with immediate international distribution (Teunissen 1992: 9). It was no coincidence that communication and fashion found each other so quickly, for fashion is based on communication. The original design could only be seen by a small elite who visited salons or were privileged enough to be admitted to the fashion show. Right from the start the general public had to get its information via a secondary medium. In the nineteenth century, the eighteenth-century fashion doll became a fashion drawing in a magazine, which then turned into fashion photographs around 1920. Now we have digital images circulating globally via the Internet in no time at all. Communication is essential for fashion, since each season a new image with new underlying ideas is produced. The public has to be informed of fashion's underlying motivation and its precise content and intention, and on the basis of analysis. For what makes something fashionable? Is it the colour yellow? Is it the length of a skirt or the use of wood and wood patterns?

Unlike traditional clothing, fashion is never based on fixed principles handed down within a particular culture. Fashion adheres to nothing. Each season it creates a completely new ambience with new interpretations that are superficially inspired or derived from fashion history, art or exotic cultures and bent to its will (Barthes 1967: 33). In order to continue understanding the constantly changing looks and their interpretations, it is necessary to provide continuous information.

After one season, the coveted wood pattern that represents a longing for 'naturalness' is pushed aside to make place for another symbol. Fashion is like the latest news. The public has to be kept informed, which is just what our modern means of communication are geared to.

THE RISE OF FASHION WEEKS

The advent of the Internet – which has been used as a medium for fashion for the past ten years or so – meant that fashion could suddenly be experienced more directly and more globally. Nowadays one can be in a remote part of Africa and follow what is happening on the fashion front in Paris (or London, Milan and New York) via the computer, while previously one had to wait for the arrival of a magazine.

This direct communication has had an enormously liberating effect. Fashion Weeks have been cropping up all over the world in the last seven years, Paris being the primary example and source of inspiration. Fashion Weeks are usually organised in various countries in order to give new local talent a chance and to promote national prosperity, as with the South Africa Fashion Week, launched in 1997. The main objective is to put one's own country on the cultural map, to support the fashion industry and to bring in a stream of tourists. Every continent now has its Fashion Weeks. Sometimes they are mainly idealistic and cultural, sometimes they exist to support commercial and sponsored enterprises. (see article on Fashion Weeks).

Until now there has been little change in the position of the West as the initiator of fashion. Paris, Milan and London still have a reputation as the most important fashion cities. What typifies these Fashion Weeks, however, is that they are all, in their own way, related to the global, international world of fashion. While they do try to link up with these international trends , they also find it important to preserve and give a place to their own traditions and culture in the field of clothing. In almost all cases fashion is linked to individual roots. This is a phenomenon unknown to Western fashion, having distanced itself since its origin from any tradition by searching constantly for the new.

LOCAL BECOMES GLOBAL

India, and in particular the Lakme Fashion Week which was initiated in 2000, is an excellent example of the different ways to relate to Western fashion on the one hand and to indigenous culture on the other. For decades India has had a film empire equal to Hollywood. India not only has a gigantic home market, but its so-called Bollywood films serve an enormous Asian market as well. The fashion industry should have a similar potential, certainly in view of the fact that for

above: STYLE.COM: forecast summer 2005
under: MANISH ARORA: a/w 2004/2005

above: SUN GODD'ESS
under: MANISH ARORA: a/w 2004/2005

centuries India has had an extensive textile industry which until recently was mainly exploited by Western companies.

Over the years an Indian design industry has gradually emerged and started to work for its own market. India has thirty million emancipated and highly trained women who are interested in fashion (Nagrath 2002: 365). Ritu Kumar, a fashion designer for almost thirty years, is someone who has built up a major brand name and has also become well-known internationally. She designs clothes for the modern Indian woman who wants to dress in the Western style but doesn't wish to abandon all the traditional items of clothing like the sari or the salwaar kameez, or the values that go with them. In this way a fusion style is created, a mixture of traditional clothing and today's trends, to a certain degree embedded in one's own culture and yet following international fashion at the same time. It is comparable with the way Muslims dress in the Netherlands and the rest of Europe. They wear a head-scarf and buttoned-up clothes because their religion requires it, but still swipe everything from the latest fashions in terms of colour, details and style. To Kumar's credit, she keeps up the custom of the sari and the salwaar kameez, items of clothing that to Western eyes are traditional and ethnic. This is not just because her female Indian patrons demand it, but also because she herself doesn't see them as ethnic garments. Her crowning glory must have been when Princess Diana appeared in a salwaar kameez during an official visit to Pakistan in 1997, thus turning it into an international fashion item. Diana bought one in an exclusive Indian couture shop in London, which has now started to attract Western customers as well.

Indian culture has been a familiar phenomenon in England for more than thirty years. It has generated its own garment industry, which in the meantime has had a springboard effect in that it has attracted the interest of Western women as well (Jones and Leskowich 2003: 5). Should the ethnic Moroccan culture develop in the same way in the Netherlands we may someday see Maxima or Mabel donning a headscarf.

GLOBAL WITH A LOCAL ACCENT

At the same time there are signs that a young generation of Indian designers, such as Malina Ramani and Manish Arora, think it is important to seek contact with Western tastes and international trends. Their main objective is to launch a global brand, but at the same time they apply their heritage and traditional Indian craftsmanship in working out and detailing their designs. Their use of Indian patterns and design elements imparts an exotic aura to fashionable clothing. Their choice of clothing forms follows a Western idiom, with a preference for sporty and casual items like T-shirts and trousers.

THE AUTO-EXOTIC GAZE

The image that exotic cultures have of themselves is often determined by the dominant West. What is Indian, after all? Is it what the people of India call Indian, or what we in the West – with our colonial past – once labelled as Indian? Dorinne Kondo's book *About Face* investigated the success of Japanese designers in Western markets in the eighties. In this connection she refers to the auto-exotic gaze that many non-Western cultures cast upon themselves. They look at their own culture with Western eyes and translate it into an 'exotic' product that they then offer back to the West (Kondo 1997: 58). A commercial example of this is the Chinese label Shanghai Tang, which opened shops a few years ago in London, Paris and Shanghai. The label tries primarily to convey a China feeling concocted entirely of clichés like embroidered satin and Shanghai Lily dresses. It packages the Chinese tradition in fashionable forms, but its main concern is to convey an authentic Chinese look with products that are thoroughly familiar in the West.

SEARCH FOR AUTHENTICITY

As this example clearly shows, the 'exotic' authenticity of a product is so important in fashion at the moment that it is turning the whole fashion hierarchy upside down. The authentic, exotic product is not being elevated to something fashionable by adapting it to current Western fashion tastes, as it previously was. The exotic product remains at the centre of attention and, with a few details, acquires a fashionable look so as to satisfy international tastes. The priority has been reversed.

What this reveals is a mentality, an attitude that can be seen among many designers at the non-Western Fashion Weeks: one's own heritage and culture have become an important stepping-off point in the design process. How does one deal with international fashion and the latest trends, and how can they be fit into one's own culture and heritage?

Even a number of Western designers – like Vivienne Westwood in England and Bernhard Wilhelm in Bavaria – base their work very clearly on their own backgrounds. The arrival of the Greek Sophia Kokasalaki in Paris last October seemed to mark a provisional high point in the longing for one's own heritage. Kokasalaki's inspiration lies in classical Greek drapery, which she translates directly into fashion with dresses that fall into supple folds. How to explain this extreme longing for authenticity? And how 'authentic' in fact is the culture that one falls back on? Greek drapery, for example, is more a mythic reference – it was worn two thousand years ago – and actually has little to do with the clothing culture and history of the Greece Kokasalaki grew up in. The question of how 'authentic' one's own cultural heritage is

above: PAUL POIRET: culotte dress 1911
under: COMME DES GARÇONS, a/w 1997/1998

above: HIPPIES DURING A LOVE-IN, England, 1967
under: ISSEY MIYAKE, a-poc camenbert, s/s 2005

seems to be one of fashion's most important sources of inspiration at the moment. And this is strange, considering the fact
that Western fashion previously looked for innovation in other
cultures rather than its own past, and was actually opposed
to traditional costume.

EXOTICISM AS SOURCE OF INNOVATION
Fashion, in the sense of constantly changing taste in clothes,
was originally a Western phenomenon, but it has always
sought inspiration in other cultures, starting with the importing of silk from China and later cotton and cashmere from
India. At that time everything was handled by Westerners,
who processed it into a product to suit Western tastes. Well-
to-do women in the Netherlands in the seventeenth and eighteenth centuries had colourful jackets made from chintz
imported from India by the Dutch East India Company. Shortly
afterwards, Indian cotton was popular in court circles for
waisted dress designs. When the fashion designer arrived in
the nineteenth century, he became the one to translate these
'exotic' fabrics and items of clothing into fashion, subjecting
the whole world to his taste.

New exotic inspirations are almost always important in
implementing a new aesthetic in fashion and in shifting
boundaries. Starting in 1908, Paul Poiret began to liberate
women from the corset and the many underskirts so as to
give their bodies an agile, supple appearance. In his eyes,
body and clothing should move in concert, as they had with
the Greeks. He saw this agility represented in the Ballet
Russes, which had recently descended on Paris, and he
became interested in all sorts of Oriental creations like the
knickerbockers that were worn in harems and reveal women's
legs – in a smart way – and show them in motion. This led
Poiret to integrate knickerbockers in his designs in all manner
of variations and combinations of shorts and skirts.

EXOTICISM AS AN AUTHENTIC PRODUCT
The 1960s saw a renewed interest in 'non-Western' clothing.
Parallel with the rise of pop music was the development of a
youth culture that repudiated fashion being imposed from
above and developed its own style by combining existing
clothes. Second-hand clothes and working men's clothing like
jeans and overalls became immensely popular, as did non-
Western items of clothing like Indian dresses, Afghan coats,
Palestinian shawls and Indian slippers. This time, for the first
time in the history of Western fashion, preferences had to do
with the romance of the unalterable 'authentic and original
product'. Just as macrobiotic food became popular in those
days as an honest, non-capitalistic nutritional choice, so too
importing authentic non-Western clothing was seen as a way
of escaping from the oppressive Western fashion culture that

imposed a new fashion norm every six months. For the first
time, fashion in those days was about correct 'styling', the
right combination of existing pieces of clothing which one
was supposed to wear without alteration (Lurie 1983: 93).
At the same moment there emerged the longing for the
'authentic', pre-industrial product that was still the result
of traditional craftsmanship, which was in danger of disap-
pearing because of the clothing industry. But it was not
until the nineties that it became the motive and source of
inspiration for both Western and non-Western designers.

PARIS BECOMES A MULTICULTURAL PLATFORM
Design and the designed garment once again became important in fashion in the early eighties with Thierry Mugler and
Claude Montana, but then something happened in Paris. A
small Japanese invasion appeared on the Parisian platform.
Kenzo, Issey Miyake and Hanae Mori had already begun in the
seventies, but when Rei Kawakubo and Yohji Yamamoto gave
their first Paris show in 1981 it caused a revolution. They
became the first non-Western designers to be included in the
official fashion world.

How were the Japanese able to gain a foothold in Paris so
quickly? Japan was already an economic power with influence in the West in the area of electronics and cars. Both
Comme des Garçons and Yamamoto had become successful
in their own countries. They had no need of the West as a
market, but decided to gain a foothold for the sake of recognition. Instead of bringing Paris down, they confirmed its importance (Kawamura 2004: 197).

The Japanese became a success because they broke all the
conventions of taste in fashion and the way it was viewed.
Their aesthetic, their taste and their way of dealing with fabric and patterns were revolutionary as well as a perfect match
for the prevailing idea of postmodernism – they were decon-
structive and they explored the boundaries of good taste, as
can be seen in the cape with holes from the 1982 Comme des
Garçons collection.

A NEW PERSPECTIVE ON CLOTHING
The sweater/cape looks worn out because it is full of holes.
For Rei Kawakubo, the designer behind Comme des Garçons,
it is no more than an experiment, a protest against the perfection of sleek, machine-made knitware. This sweater therefore
has a random pattern of holes, which immediately makes the
outfit multi-functional and wearable in several ways (Kondo
1997: 58). Apparently, the fact that the sweater has no fixed
form is also a typical Japanese design principle. At the same
time, the Japanese put a great deal of emphasis on the fabric,
giving it a new look by using all manner of ancient Japanese

COMME DES GARÇONS, lacework sweater, 1982

manufacturing techniques – tie and dye, pleating, matting, etc. (Fukai 2003: 22). The sweater with holes looks almost anti-aesthetic to our eyes, but Issey Miyake's world famous and very practical Pleats Please line is an ultramodern product based on an ancient Japanese principle of pleating, but produced in a technologically advanced way. Miyake considers it important to retain and use traditional craftsmanship and handicraft traditions. 'The only way to achieve this is by making tradition modern through technology. If we cannot make traditions suitable for today's lifestyle in function and price then the traditions will eventually die out.' (Holborn 1995: 104)

The extent to which Miyake's designs are imbued with Japanese traditions is also apparent in the way fabric is dealt with. The approach to fabric in Japan is not only extremely ingenious, but fabric itself is traditionally so sacred that you can not just cut it any way you want. And if you do, then at least you have to be as economical as possible. In 1999 this mentality resulted in A-POC (A Piece of Cloth), the latest Issey Miyake line, which he still always designs himself. Here the finished item of clothing is already incorporated into the fabric and only has to be cut loose. This is made possible by means of a brand-new moulding technology, but the principle goes back to the ancient idea of being economical with fabric.

PATTERNS VS FOLDS
Being economical with fabric also means there is more folding and playing with volumes than working with patterns and cutting. Whereas fashion in the West has been based for centuries on creating and recreating an ideal silhouette, the Japanese clothing tradition is based on the straight length of cloth of the kimono and on folding. In 1999 Yamamoto designed a collection in which he played with the then current revival of haute couture. He added new forms and volumes to tight, body-hugging designer bodices by attaching loose pieces of cloth to them, thus exploring how East and West can merge in a single new creation.

Not only can Japanese creations be worn in several ways, but they often are also surprisingly asymmetrical, and that goes in particular for Yamamoto. Symmetry is the symbol of perfection, but in his view it is 'inhuman' (Teunissen 2001: 83).

JAPANESE TRADITION AS POSTMODERNISM
As already mentioned, all these new approaches were interpreted in the eighties as examples of postmodern deconstruction. An investigation by Rei Kawakubo from Commes des Garçons into what precisely is functional and decorative in clothing by making the functional decorative and vice versa, is indeed a postmodernist game with meaning, but one that

is actually prompted by his own Japanese background and not by Western postmodernism.

The Japanese introduced a great many new fashion ideas in the eighties. The idea is not to create a Japanese 'atmosphere' but to undertake an analysis of clothing in the form of clothing, based on a great many traditional Japanese elements. At that time, in the early eighties, there was an enormous amount of innovation in fashion. Western fashion suddenly became conceptual and analytic and, as in the period of Paul Poiret, there emerged a fresh new aesthetic and new limits to work within. The last twenty years have shown how much Yamamoto, Commes des Garçons and Miyake have influenced a new generation of designers like Martin Margiela, Viktor & Rolf and Hussein Chalayan.

A NEW PERSPECTIVE ON THE BODY
The Japanese designers also gave a new definition to notions of masculinity and femininity. The idea of 'sexy' does not appear in the Japanese fashion vocabulary. Through the consistent use of flat shoes, abstract make-up and walking in an 'ordinary' way during the shows, the models always look androgynous and abstract. This means that the clothes can be worn much more naturally by young and old, Asiatic and Western, than would be the case with a Versace outfit. (Kondo 1997: 59)

Japanese designers actually broke through the Western modernist aesthetic that had determined everything up until that time. Before then it had always been a quest for the ultimate and sublime silhouette, like Christian Dior's New Look in 1947 or Courreges space look in 1964.

AFRICA IN THE PICTURE
Not only were the boundaries of the fashion system thrown open in the eighties, but Paris too, as a platform, turned its gaze outward in the hope of incorporating even more influence from non-Western cultures, which would break through the boundaries and values of Western fashion in another fruitful way.

Around ten years later another non-Westerner made his mark on the Parisian fashion stage: Lamine Kouyaté from Mali, who in 1992 introduced the label Xuly Bet. Kouyate came to France to study architecture, but he finally chose the fashion trade. His designs were initially made from second-hand clothes that he bought in flea markets, unstitched and then sewed together again arbitrarily, preferably with the seams on the outside. Nowadays there are a lot of idealistic companies working this way, but back then it was revolutionary, mainly because he coupled it with bizarre presentations – disturb-

above: CHRISTIAN DIOR, New Look, 1947
under: HUSSEIN CHALAYAN, In Between, a/w 1998

above: ANDRÉ COURRÈGES, Moongirl, 1964
under: HUSSEIN CHALAYAN, Ambimorphous, a/w 2002/2003

ances in the Paris metro – and very much with the music world and the ethnic youth scene.

POLITICAL CONTRIBUTION

The Turkish Cypriot designer Hussein Chalayan (born in Nicosia in 1970) also bears the aura of a non-Western designer. A crucial moment in his career was the veils collection he showed at the London Fashion Week in 1998. The first models in the collection entered fully veiled, but the hem lengths of the ones that followed became shorter and shorter, until the final model appeared wearing nothing but a mask. Chalayan's collection is in fact a highly formal investigation of seeing and being seen, but at the same time the series can be regarded as a commentary on Muslim culture. How Chalayan deals with his own past is also evident in the presentation of Afterwards (2000), an installation representing the refugee's existence in a Cyprus divided into Greek and Turkish parts.

Traditional clothing is beautifully highlighted in Chalayan's *Ambimorphous* collection (a/w 2002), which is based on Turkish/Mongolian costumes. With part of the complicated creation always executed in black, its stratification becomes visible. The result of this formal investigation is that the black, wearable creations reveal a splendid, abstract interplay of lines.

AUTHENTICITY AS ROMANTIC IDEA

Both Lamine Kouyaté and Hussein Chalayan are innovative in their attitude towards fashion, but they have changed the fashion system and ideas about fashion less radically than the Japanese. What both of them have done, however, is provide fashion with a new mentality: Kouyaté by re-using existing clothing and in the vital way he reunites it with urban culture, and Chalayan mainly by weaving his own history into his designs as a politically laden story. It is noteworthy that, in both cases, the press and critics make much of their 'exotic' background. But whether this is really so important in terms of design techniques is open to doubt. Rather, their non-European background adds a dose of romanticism or authenticity to their designs. Both of them do make use of their origins as a source of inspiration and in producing their designs, which are certainly imbued in one way or another with local craftsmanship and tradition.

HOLDING ON TO ONE'S OWN HERITAGE

Reflecting on one's own heritage also plays a role among Western designers. In the work of Vivienne Westwood, for example, we observe an important transformation in the early nineties. Until then, this English designer was mainly known as the Queen of Punk. She dressed the Sex Pistols and ran her famous London shops, Sex and Seditionaries. But in the

nineties she suddenly dived into English costume history, devoting herself to tailored jackets, English checks, the baseball shirt and almost everything that had to do with the English fashion past. All sorts of symbols and signs relating to the Royal Family or the aristocratic country life of former times turned up on logos, bags and perfume. For Westwood it was all a question of nostalgia, the idea that her own tradition and the craftsmanship of English clothesmakers should not be allowed to vanish because of the fashion industry, which levels everything out (Jonkers 2003:18).

A similar form of sentimentality can be seen with Barnhard Wilhelm. Trained in Antwerp but originally from the German city of Ulm, Wilhelm adopts a mix and match style, making full use of traditional crafts and things associated with do-it-yourself fashion. He names his mother, a Bavarian housewife, as an important source of inspiration. She crochets and knits all sorts of things for him, then sends them to him, and if he likes them he'll use them in his collections for socks, shawls and pieces of embroidery. Wilhelm is mainly interested in the handiwork feeling and the do-it-yourself principles of the seventies. He doesn't restrict himself to Bavarian inspiration, but selects pictures and comic strips from all over the world, which he then embroiders, crochets or sews onto his garments.

Finally, there's the already mentioned Sophia Kokolasaki from Greece, who studied at St Martins Royal College of Art and Design in London and quickly achieved fame with her shows at the London Fashion Week. Presenting herself last October in Paris, she was embraced by the press as the very latest talent. At the moment nobody symbolises the theme of Global Fashion, Local Tradition more literally than Kokolasaki. The ties with the past are becoming more and more direct in Western fashion, and the longing for 'authenticity' is extraordinarily great. A last, less well-known example of this is the Russian Razu Mikhina, who has chosen Milan as her headquarters for the time being and bases her designs on Russian crafts. Clearly, as her rustic-looking photographs confirm, her wish is to give the Russian tradition of lace and ribbons a place in the future.

LIFESTYLE

How far will we go in promoting and propagating our own local crafts in the future? Why has there been such a great need since the eighties to anchor fashion in one's own culture? With the rise of lifestyle in the eighties, even major companies and commercial brands have started to exploit their national identity. Oilily in The Netherlands began in the seventies as a jolly children's label, its use of patchwork a clear reference to traditional Dutch costume. In the meantime

above: VIVIENNE WESTOOD, Dressing up, 1991
under: RAZU MIKHINA: a/w 2003/2004

above : BERNHARD WILLHELM s/s 2004
under: OILILY s/s 2004

Oilily has grown into a global brand whose image continues to be determined by lively patterns and designs, but these are no longer strictly of Dutch origin. Also conspicuous are the American companies that convey an America feeling and succeed in narrating an authentic image of America that is different each time. Ralph Lauren depicts America as a country with an aristocratic culture, a past that it has actually never known. Tommy Hilfiger sketches an image of a preppy and functional America, while Levi's has long romanticised the colonial farming past. Always the same America, yet totally different. So companies also feel they have to link their image to their background. (see: Ted Polhemus)

FASHION AS SUPER-SAMPLING

The obsession with authenticity and crafts traditions has been visible for a number of years in John Galliano's work. Galliano, designer for Dior and responsible for a label of his own, travels all over the world like a modern explorer. He collects books, clothes and unusual things he comes across on his travels and sends them to Paris, where a team begins using them in designs. On his return he transforms all the experiences he has undergone on his travels into unique, over-the-top creations, incorporating influences from costume history and tramps' carts as well as Eastern European and Asiatic crafts into a wonderful mix and match of styles.

Galliano sees the world as a grab bag of possibilities, filled with numerous visual styles that can be used at random. He does what has always been done in fashion, symbolising what fashion essentially is: an eclectic, opportunistic and ephemeral medium. In this age of globalisation, communication and endless accessibility, he expands this eclecticism into a super-sampling of styles. 'What's modern? I think re-interpreting things with today's influences, today's fabric technology, is what it is all about.' (Frankel 2001: 170)

Nobody would really walk across the street in one of his extravagant crinolines, nor would the designer expect them to. What he's trying to say is that right now one gets from fashion what one wants. Just as you bring back souvenirs of your holiday, so you take what you like from the fancy dress box of Western fashion history and create your own combinations.

ETHICAL FASHION VS ECLECTICISM

With Galliano, too, we see a fascination with craftsmanship and clothing traditions from other cultures. His reason for deploying them is that he is interested in local dress customs, and in the skill and expertise involved, purely because of the craftsmanship. Galliano loves technique, crafts and refinement, but applies them in his own way. He is not interested in anything like an 'authentic' past, and although he does some-times bring his own Spanish background into play, this is not what characterises his style, nor is it the guiding principle in his designs. Galliano represents fashion in the classical sense, the way it always was, as an exhausted carnival of sampled ideas. This is what makes him diametrically opposed to a new category of fashion designers who put their own background and the craftsmanship that comes from their clothing culture first and foremost.

ONE'S OWN ROOTS

How much this latter aspect is becoming important is indeed evident in the attention a number of local initiatives are currently receiving in the fashion world at large. With their small-scale production methods and ancient techniques they are succeeding in becoming part of the international fashion industry in a particular way. What is making this possible is the fact that they have a website and are able to promote themselves as international labels via their own country's or continent's fashion week.

An example of such an initiative is Dene Fur Clouds, a community of 700 Canadian Indians who live in a culture whose ecology is balanced and consciously maintained. The fur of the animals they eat is used for clothing. The wool is finger-knitted into fur-lined sweaters, bonnets and capes. The capes and sweaters, with their authentic Nomad look, have been selling like wildfire since they appeared on the Internet and were shown at the Toronto Fashion Week and even in Paris with Fur Works Canada.

Coopa Roca, a women's cooperative from Rocinha near Rio de Janeiro, is trying to preserve and spread traditional Brazilian handicrafts. Set up in the eighties as a women's initiative, it enables women to easily combine childcare and work. In the meantime there are 150 members, providing services to Brazilian designers as well as to the South American branch of C&A.

In Mexico we find Pineda Covalin, which mainly concentrates on colour patterns in fabrics based on ancient Pre-Columbian and Mexican traditions. This enterprise does not represent the efforts of a local or authentic population but of two idealistic designers who took part in a few workshops with the local inhabitants in an attempt at to bring back traditional crafts. They mainly distribute their products via the museum circuit.

On the basis of a similar ideological background, the Chinese designer Shirley Yeung Laam recently inaugurated her China Lane label. After studying fashion design at Parsons in New York she spent a few years as a fashion buyer for large stores. She now uses the knowledge and the network thus acquired

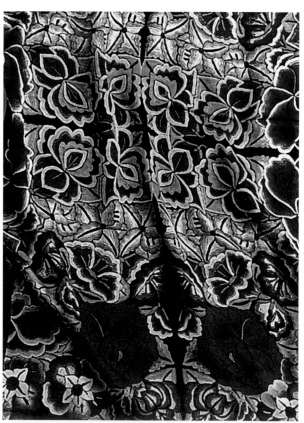

above: JOHN GALLIANO, a/w 2004/2005
under: DENE FUR CLOUDS, a/w 2003/2004

above: DENE FUR CLOUDS, a/w 2004/2005
under: PINEDA COVALIN, accessory line 2005

to offer the Maobe tribe in Central China a better life. She has them weave and embroider traditional Chinese silk in a classical way. Shirley Yeung first came up with a home-wear collection, but now she has a small pret-à-porter line which she sells in Paris. In this she combines embroidered silk jackets with cashmere sweaters that are also produced and woven by the Maobe tribe. To make these items more fashionable she then combines them with jeans adorned here and there with small pieces of embroidery. So China Lane is another label with a strong idealistic background that is achieving success via the international fashion market in Paris.

AND NOW?

Why is fashion so preoccupied with returning to tradition at the present moment? Is it to play a game with tradition and to extract knowledge from it, as John Galliano is doing? Is drawing innovation from it the most important motive, as the Japanese have convincingly shown in the last twenty years? Or are there more romantic reasons as well? Because of the advance of the fashion industry in the sixties and the shifting of production to low-wage countries, clothing products have lost their quality. These are the important motives for Vivienne Westwood and Issay Miyake. They are afraid that with large-scale production we are in danger of losing traditional knowledge and craftsmanship.

Or is it the need for individuality and an identity of one's own in a world in which H&M is omnipresent as the hamburger of fashion? Or is it perhaps the need to escape from the fickleness of fashion? Producing something different every six months is exhausting, after all. And that aura of 'the temporary' attaches much less to an authentic product. Such a product has something timeless about it; one doesn't readily throw it away. What's more, the craftsmanship contained within it makes it a high-quality product, not just a throw-away article. This quality is what we find important at the moment.

REDEFINING CONCEPTS

We can, at any rate, conclude that fashion as a concept is in need of redefinition. Fashion is no longer a Western, hierarchical system that defines what good taste is and how it can be imitated. Fashion was already democratised in the 1900s. It was no longer the couturiers and the elite who decided what the latest fashion was, but youth culture and the street. Now a similar turn seems to be in motion. It is no longer the West that prescribes fashion; it can arise anywhere on earth and find a place in the international fashion world.

Traditional cultures are playing a greater part in the game of fashion than is generally thought, as the example of India illustrates. They too are blurring the boundaries between tra-

ditional clothing and fashion in all manner of ways. The work of the artist Roy Villevoye illustrates very well how 'genuinely' authentic cultures that are not familiar at all with the phenomenon of fashion still incorporate fashion elements naturally in their culture. The collection of Villevoye's photographs further on in this book illustrates how the Asmat people in Papua New Guinea have incorporated the T-shirt into their clothing and adornment culture. The Asmats live a very isolated existence and still take care of their basic necessities in an authentic way. With no money economy, they exchange things whenever they encounter Westerners. Villevoye discovered that they have a preference for T-shirts which they treat in their own way, scrawling on them the same way they scrawl on their bodies. We, as Westerners, are unable to follow exactly what the meanings are, but what is interesting is that they, too, are open to influences from outside.

As this example makes clear, we need to review our classical ideas about fashion. Traditional clothing cultures are also open to change and are less fixed and enduring than anthropologists have always thought.

There remains the question as to what exactly fashion is nowadays and who actually defines it? Will we get more regional fashions in the future? How important is the longing for one's own heritage? Is 'authenticity' simply a fashionable phenomenon that will go away by itself? Or, with the emancipation of different continents in the area of fashion, will it remain an important reference? Ted Polhemus demonstrates that major labels usually cannot ignore their own identity and background if they want to build a worldwide image. Will it also continue to be important for non-Western designers to include their roots as a vital part of their label's image?

Time will tell.

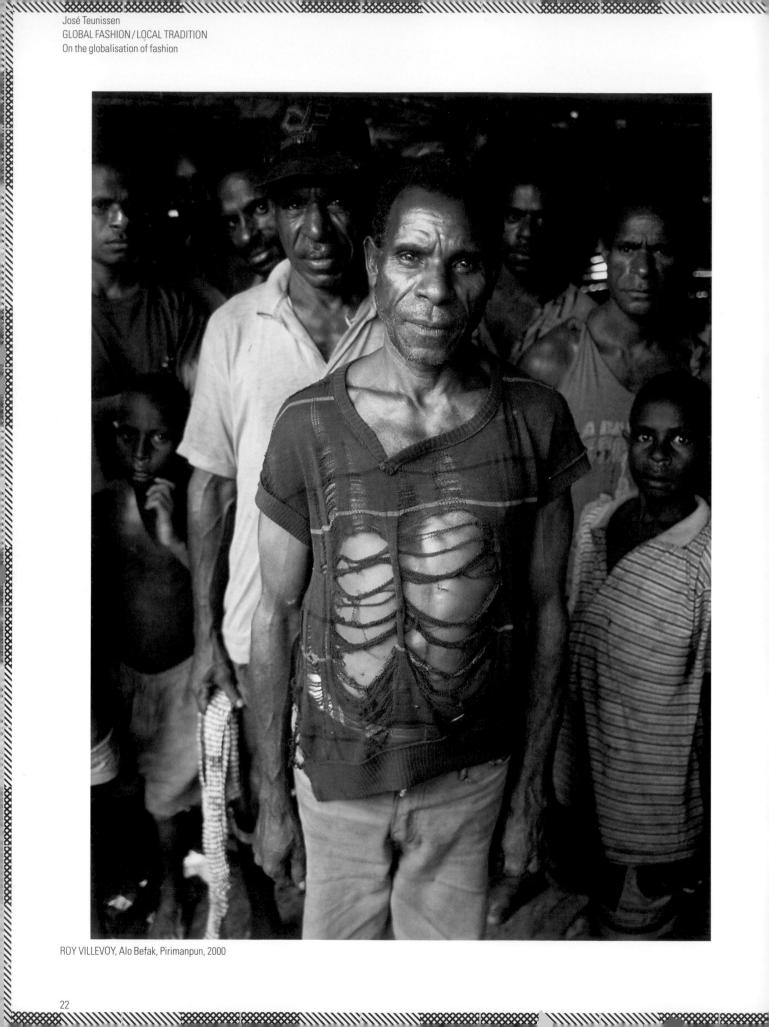

ROY VILLEVOY, Alo Befak, Pirimanpun, 2000

REFERENCES:

Barthes, Roland. – SYSTÈME DE LA MODE – Paris: Editions de seuil, 1967.

Craik, Jennifer – THE FACE OF FASHION – London: Routledge, 1994.

Frankel, Susannah – VISIONAIRIES – London, V&A publications. 2001.

Fukai, Akiko – 'Le Japon et le Mode', in: XXIÈME CIEL. MODE IN JAPAN – Nice: Musee des Arts Asiatique, 2003, pp. 21-27.

Holborn, Mark – ISSEY MIYAKE – Cologne: Taschen Verlag, 1995.

Jones and Leskowich – RE-ORIENTING FASHION – Oxford: Berg, 2003

Jonkers, Gert – 'Vivienne Westwood', in: Brand, Jan and Teunissen José, WOMAN BY – Utrecht: Centraal Museum. 2003

Kawamura, Yunija – 'The Japanese revolution in Paris Fashion', in: FASHION THEORY 8 – New York: Berg Publishers, June 2004.

Kondo, Dorinne – ABOUT FACE: PERFORMING RACE IN FASHION AND THEATRE – London: Routledge, 1997.

Lurie, Alison – THE LANGUAGE OF CLOTHES – London: Hamlyn, 1983.

Nagrath, Sumati – '(En)countering Orientalism in High Fashion: A Review of India Fashion Week 2002', FASHION THEORY 7 – issue 3-4 (2003).

Teunissen, José – MADE IN JAPAN – Utrecht: Centraal Museum, 2001.

Susannah Frankel
ANYTHING GOES

From pirate fantasies to Russian folk art, the collision of influences that goes into a JOHN GALLIANO creation makes each one unique.

John Galliano says that his autumn/winter 2004 collection is 'a seafaring adventure', inspired in particular by the not entirely seafaring Yemen tribespeople who wear all their worldly possessions on their bodies at any one given time. Certainly, to describe the look as eclectic would be an understatement. But then the designer pretty much invented the mix-and-match style that continues to rule the runways. For the past twenty-odd years he has grabbed at references from the world over, throwing them together with an irreverent abandon that remains unparalleled despite having spawned a million imitations. Above all, Galliano loves colour – a result, no doubt, of his background.

Born and christened Juan Carlos Antonio, in Gibraltar – his father's homeland – the designer's mother is Spanish. 'I lived in Gibraltar until I was six, so I travelled a lot.' To go to school in Spain, for example, he passed through Tangiers – an exotic journey if ever there was one for a small boy with a passion for all things rainbow-hued. 'I think all that – the souks, the markets, woven fabrics, the carpets, the smells, the herbs, the Mediterranean colour – is where my love of textiles comes from,' he explains.

Whichever way you choose to look at it, there can only be a few examples of his work to rival the one photographed here in embodying not only a love of vibrant fabric but also the blending of myriad influences – geographical and, indeed, historical.

Beginning with the skirt – surely the biggest and brightest of its kind in fashion history. 'It was made from old scarves bought in Barbes [in Paris's 18th arrondissement],' Galliano says. 'We recycled them and mixed them with hand-made strips of boiled and felted wool. It is also padded and has a cartridge pleated waist.' The jacket is made of linen, 'block printed with a design taken from a Russian tray'. The corset is Victorian inspired, ruffled and embroidered with gold and silver coins. Beneath it all is a grey marle jump suit – designed to keep our heroine warm, no doubt. Finally, of course, there are the shoes, forgotten beneath the huge floral folds but most surely worth a mention nonetheless. They are little lace-up granny boots with the now classic Galliano newsprint design stamped on to the soles; the colours of the left and right foot don't quite match, which only exaggerates the hobo-esque – even slightly touched – feel of the whole.

As always, the headwear, a result of Galliano's ten-year collaboration with the milliner Stephen Jones, drives home the designer's message of the season. In this case, we have Mr Jones to thank for larger-than-life-size, plaited woollen wigs, embellished with plastic coins that are dip-dyed silver. (More elaborate examples still had silver knives and forks dangling from their ebony coils.)

Galliano has, in the past, been criticised for putting looks such as this one on to his catwalk, given that it is unlikely that the exact style will ever go into mass production. 'Fashion is about excitement and change,' the designer explains. 'If you don't challenge people, fashion will not change. One example is the bias-cut dress.' This, above all else, is, of course, a Galliano signature. 'But when we first presented it, the accepted rule was that it couldn't be produced industrially so we had to have the dresses made with a company that produces theatre costumes. Now, not only can the dresses be produced industrially but they are everywhere – on the high street as well as in the designers' collections.'

The jacket shown here is 'one of this season's best sellers', he argues, produced in ten different fabrics and in the same shape, 'but not cut on a corset'. The corset has also been commercialised, although, perhaps sadly, the coins haven't made it onto the rails. 'As for the skirt,' says the designer, 'it was a show piece', also used for display in the Paris store.

All in all, this just goes to prove that only the bold dare to wear John Galliano – in anything from its most extreme to its most ready-to-wear incarnation. And that is precisely the point. Shrinking violets would do well to shop elsewhere, thank you. Instead, this great British fashion talent creates clothes that are, in his own words, 'full of fantasy, fun, eclecticism and that embody a piratical approach to fashion'.

Nobody does it better.

JOHN GALLIANO, a/w 2004/2005

JOHN GALLIANO, a/w 2004/2005

Anne van der Zwaag

FASHION WEEKS

Iceland FW

Russian FW

Russian FW

Toronto FW
Montréal FW
London FW
Amsterdam FW
Austrian FW
Posnan FW
Romanian FW

San Francisco FW
New York FW
Paris FW
Milan FW
Zagreb FW
Portugal FW
Barcelona FW
Sarajevo FW
Seoul FW
Tokyo FW
Madrid FW

Los Angeles FW
Caribean FW
FW of the America's
Saigon FW
Hong Kong FW
Lakmé India FW
Colombia FW
Kuala Lumpur FW
Singapore FW
Jakarta FW
Bali FW
Rio de Janeiro FW
São Paulo FW
New Zealand FW
South African FW
Santiago FW
Buenos Aires FW
Australian FW

above: MAP
under right: LONDON FASHION WEEK   under left: MILAN FASHION WEEK

The Amsterdam International Fashion Week took place in Amsterdam for the first time in the summer of 2004. The idea was to put Amsterdam on the map as an international fashion destination. Nowadays fashion weeks are held all over the world. Countries like the United States, Iceland, Singapore, South Africa, Russia, Malaysia and New Zealand all have their own fashion weeks, sometimes even several. This map of the world gives an impression of the current extent of the phenomenon. The number is continually growing, however, so the map in no way pretends to be complete. In one year, 2004, fashion weeks were inaugurated in Amsterdam, Helsinki and San Francisco, undoubtedly in imitation of cities traditionally associated with couture such as Paris, Milan, New York and London, where the fashion week has already been an institution for decades.

ICONS

These prestigious fashion weeks have comparable goals and a largely similar organisational structure. Every two years they present the latest summer and winter collections. One indispensable element is a so-called *fashion council*, a federation responsible for setting up and directing the fashion week. The council is a non-profit organisation made up of representatives from the fashion branch . The goal they set themselves is to centralise and organise the field of fashion in order to bring the media, retailers and buyers in contact with the best of what their country has to offer. 'The Camera Nazionale della Moda Italiana is a non-profit organisation for streamlining, coordinating and promoting Italian fashion. The organisation represents the very best in Italian fashion. Its aim is to protect, coordinate and strengthen the image of Italian fashion – both in Italy and abroad,' write the Milanese organisers. Although the activities of the fashion councils are supported financially by companies in the fashion industry for the most part, it is important to attract a major sponsor. Sponsoring makes it possible to offer a location and high-quality facilities so the organisers can then attract national as well as international top designers. These fashion weeks more or less owe their status to companies like l'Oréal or Mercedes-Benz. The New York Fashion Week, founded in 1993, is entirely supported by corporate sponsors. Since 2004 the camera brand Olympus has been the title sponsor of the fashion week, which has now been renamed 'Olympus Fashion Week'.

An impressive list of participants is typical of these sorts of fashion weeks. Besides major American labels like Donna Karan, Calvin Klein and Ralph Lauren, top foreign designers such as Caroline Herrera and Oscar de la Renta show in New York. The fashion presented here is predominantly uniform. The London Fashion Week, on the other hand, is geared more to innovation. If there is a pecking order among them, then New York probably ranks as the most commercial. But it is not only the big names that participate in these fashion weeks. Each season brings with it national and international designers who may well enjoy a reputation in their own country but for whom an invitation from Paris, Milan, New York or London represents the ultimate recognition, as well as opportunity to get a leg up in the Western fashion world and market. The organisers have taken this step because the competition from alternative fashion destinations is becoming greater and greater. To maintain their image as trendsetters they have to roll up their sleeves. For many years the position of these fashion weeks was unrivalled, but loss of status seemed inevitable. For although Paris and Milan are still seen as the centre of fashion, fashion weeks nowadays are imitating them and taking place all over the world. Does this mean that the hegemony of Western fashion is coming to an end? In this essay I explain how fashion weeks arose and what their nature is, and why the advent of this phenomenon is having such a major impact on the concept of fashion as dictated by the West.

NEW VANGUARD

A category of fashion weeks has arisen that is very different from all the major models, and the organisers are aware of this. 'The Amsterdam International Fashion Week is steadily establishing itself as a young and directional alternative to the world's more traditional fashion weeks,' claim the organisers of the event in The Netherlands. These fashion weeks are relatively young and, in contrast to the major players in the field, are usually organised or supported by local government, relying only secondarily on support from commercial sponsors. Instead of depending on an impressive international line-up, this type of fashion week is characterised by experiment and innovation. The organisers are hoping to discover a new generation of innovative fashion designers and to introduce them in their own country, possibly as a step towards the continental or inter-continental fashion industry. 'Our aim is to contribute to the development of the Portuguese textile and fashion industry and to the worldwide promotion of Portuguese products, companies and designers', is how a spokesperson describes the goals of Portugal Fashion. From this we can conclude that the reason for organising this fashion week is the need to professionalise the national fashion industry internally and to improve its profile externally. The same goes for all the fashion weeks in this category. The Official Calendar of Brazilian Fashion, the body behind the São Paulo fashion week, was set up in order to bring together the nation's textile industries and to make Brazilian fashion stronger, more professional and more visible. Paulo Borges, creative director of the São Paulo Fashion Week, describes their aim as follows: 'It has always been my firm conviction

SOUTH AFRICAN FASHION WEEK 2004
above: DARKIE
under: STONED CHERRIE

NEW YORK FASHION WEEK 2005
above: RALPH LAUREN
under: DONNA KAREN

SÂO PAULO FASHION WEEK 2004
above : COOPA-ROCA
under : ALEXANDRE HERCHCOVITCH

that the only way we can strengthen the fashion industry in Brazil is by taking stock of all its aspects together and in an organised way. In a country like ours, which is as big as a continent, we need a trendsetting centre if we want to expand our overseas trade. We have to be able to show the same power and infrastructure as other major fashion-producing countries.'

In May 1999, at the request of more than twenty Latin American designers, Beth Sobol launched the comparable Fashion Week of the Americas, specifically aimed at putting fashion designers on the map from Latin America and the Caribbean. Although fashion weeks are usually initiated by a fashion council, this is not the case here. Not long after the founding of the event, however, the importance of such a federation was indeed recognised. In that same year, at the initiative of the leading Venezuelan designer Caroline Herrera, the Council of Latin American Fashion Designers was set up, akin to the councils in Paris and Milan. Like them, it is an organisation that strives to establish a bridge between regional designers and the fashion industry by promoting them as international instead of as 'folklore'. The Singapore Fashion Week, in its eighteen years of existence, has proved that the gulf between East and West can indeed be bridged. This fashion week attracts many young designers from Singapore and the region. And not for nothing. The large-scale nature of the event and the presence of a considerable number of international buyers from the United States, Canada and Japan has turned the Singapore Fashion Week into a genuine hub of the international market.

As Beth Sobol makes clear, the success of these initiatives is due to the increasing globalisation of society. 'As our global community becomes more cohesive we see fewer and fewer boundaries as we embrace each other's cultures, integrating them into our own, yet retaining our own distinctive style and essence.' Harleen Sabharwal, trend forecaster from India, observes a comparable development which she calls 'glocalisation'. A new form of fusion fashion is coming about, a mixture of global and traditional influences. And indeed, Western designers, with John Galliano in the forefront, are willingly influenced by native and local traditions, materials and patterns. At the same time, non-Western designers are becoming aware of the success of a Tommy Hilfiger or Zara, and as a result are increasingly supplying the local population with a regionally inspired look that has been given a global face-lift.

SHOWPIECES
In fact these sorts of fashion weeks function not only as a signboard for national fashion but also as ambassadors for the country itself, which is very clearly reflected in the goals of the Kuala Lumpur-Asia Fashion Week. The primary aim of the fashion week is to create new trade possibilities for the country. In my view, the fact that these initiatives are supported by governments worldwide has everything to do with this. It's a matter here of a form of nation branding in that a clear and positive economic stimulus stems from the events. Dame Cheryll Sotheran, Sector Director, Creative Industries, New Zealand Trade and Enterprise, underlines this: 'Governments around the Asia-Pacific region – in Australia, Malaysia, Singapore and Hong Kong – are all supporting fashion weeks. They see these events as high-profile branding opportunities for their country and work to leverage events and focus international attention on their successes.' Pieter Stewart has been organising the event since 2001, with the support of New Zealand Trade and Enterprise, Tourism New Zealand, Tourism Auckland and Auckland City. 'In a global economy dominated by brands, New Zealand's creative industries – from fashion to film, design and music – all play a major part in raising New Zealand's visibility. This makes our fashion designers ambassadors for New Zealand on the world stage. Having consumers overseas wearing New Zealand labels, seeing influential media, buyers, even celebrities talking about our designers, is the sort of endorsement that makes New Zealand a talking point and has positive spillovers for all our exports,' continues Cheryll. Not surprisingly, the fashion week here is fully focused on supporting and promoting New Zealand designers. In the Netherlands, the Amsterdam International Fashion Week is likewise supported by the government. The Amsterdam City Council's economic action programme 'HERMEZ' (Het Economisch Resultaat Moet Er Zijn – Economic Results are Indispensable) makes a contribution to the event. And here too the fashion week functions as a national commercial. As Alderman Huffnagel puts it, 'Promoting the city is one of the cornerstones of the Hermez action programme. The Fashion Week makes a positive contribution to raising Amsterdam's international visibility as a fashion city. The interest of all the foreign media means that the Fashion Week can be regarded as a foreign trade mission in our own country.'

The organisational structure and aims of the fashion weeks are often similar, but this does not mean that the setup is always the same. The events tend to differ in terms of content, which makes it difficult to divide them into sub-categories. Some events incorporate foreign participants, others are restricted to national designers. Most fashion weeks are internationally oriented, but there are also fashion weeks geared to the local market. It is striking, however, that the success of the initiative does not depend on it being Western or non-Western. What is of crucial importance is the development of a national fashion industry. If such an industry scarce-

JOHN GALLIANO

ly exists, then the fashion week is primarily aimed at stimulating it and creating a market for it. The step onto the global stage is simply too great here. Countries that have long had a flourishing textile industry need to promote themselves internationally all the more. In this case there is already an infrastructure present, which makes it easier to produce, distribute and sell the collections at home as well as abroad.

TESTBED
Almost all the 'alternative' fashion weeks are breeding grounds for undiscovered talent – international talent in some cases. The Russian Fashion Week in 2004 presented more than sixty designers from various countries including Russia, the Baltic States, Georgia, England, The Netherlands, France, Spain, Peru, Indonesia and the Ukraine. It was dominated by experiments. The Russians have a tradition of avant-gardism, and this could be seen on the catwalks, which were populated by unconventional, upcoming designers like the Russian Razu Mikhina and Nota Bene & Karavay from the Ukraine. The fashion week in Iceland is less ambitious but at least as diverse, testifying to just as much passion for experiment. During this annual event, relatively unknown designers from all over the world show their ready-to-wear and haute couture collections – and with success. Jay Levine of Fashion Television excitedly called Reykjavik Fashion 'a world-class show'. The Russian Fashion Week and Reykjavik Fashion may have an international look, but the priority is always to promote local labels.

The Kuala Lumpur-Asia Fashion Week likewise focuses on young potential, promoting upcoming regional designers and developing the local fashion scene. Similarly, the South African Fashion Week represents a genuine reflection of the collective fashion talent in South Africa. Here collections are presented of labels that are quite new to us, such as Stoned Cherry and Darkie, which mix African and Western influences in an experimental way. The South African Fashion Week may still be aimed at the national market, but it is a country that indisputably wants to measure up to the West. The international ambition of its organisers can clearly be seen in the fact that they recruited L'Oreal Paris as sponsor in 2004 and chose South African Oscar winner Charlize Theron as the face of that year's campaign. More than anyone else, she embodies the worldwide success of South African talent. Partly because of this, the event will most likely gain global recognition.

The Lakmé India Fashion Week supplies India with a type of fashion that is representative of its own culture and is also chic. Michael Fink of New York's Saks Fifth Avenue observes, 'Indian designers are as good or bad as any around the world and they should be encouraged for the wonderful work they are doing in fusing ancient traditions into modern clothes.' India has had a rich textile heritage since time immemorial, but fashion design as an industry is still young. Yet the fashion branch is rapidly expanding. With the recent growth of the Indian economy, there is a growing demand for affordable prêt-à-porter clothing. The fashion week takes advantage of this by offering both ready-to-wear and 'diffusion'. Because of the large retail market, the fashion week has grown considerably in the past years, and in magnitude the event is a match for Paris or Milan. Not only is there is a great deal of interest in Indian designers in India itself, but in other countries there is also growing appreciation for what India has to offer. Thus the twenty-nine-year-old Sabyasachi Mukherjee showed for the first time in Milan in the autumn of 2004, proof of the power of fusion fashion. He deliberately decided on an Indian-inspired Western look. 'There was no traditional silhouette of India – no saris, no sarongs, it was all very international. But I get incredibly inspired by the warm tones of India,' which he himself calls 'Indianised'. In any case there seems to be a lot afoot in India, since European designers like Cavalli and Armani are also looking for inspiration there. After a number of visits to the East, Giorgio Armani is thinking about trying to conquer the Indian market. The other way round, major Western department stores Browns and Saks are showing an interest in Indian designers like Mukherjee. His eye remains focused for the time being on India, his home base. 'I think that while the Western market is full of all kinds of designer labels, the Asiatic market is naive, experimental and flourishing, and thus extremely lucrative in a commercial respect,' and the same goes for a great many Indian designers.

GROWING PAINS
Not all fashion weeks are success stories. Because of Communist influence, designers from the Soviet region have lived in a vacuum for decades, and this has largely determined the development in the Russian fashion industry. Both the designers as well as the Russian public saw fashion as an art form, which resulted in fanciful but unwearable designs. And even if the designs were wearable, the collections were seldom taken into production. A fundamental problem in Russia was the lack of professionalism among the designers. The Russian Fashion Week was established in 2002 and the organisers initially attracted a large number of foreign designers, partly as a way of inciting Russian fashion designers to move into production. Only in the past few years has there been an active generation of designers making wearable garments aimed at a broad public. Now that the tide has turned we are starting to get an impression of the enormous potential hidden away in that nation. But has the Russian public also undergone a change of mentality? A poll among visitors to the Russian Fashion Week in the spring of 2004 revealed that 46 percent

AMSTERDAM INTERNATIONAL FASHION WEEK 2004
above: CATRIN NEYER

RUSSIAN FASHION WEEK 2005
above: VERONIKA SAMBORSKAYA
under: NOTA BENE & KARAVAY

LAKMÉ INDIA FASHION WEEK 2004
above: SABYASACHI MUKHERJEE
under: MANISH ARORA

still prefer international labels including Gucci, Armani, Dolce & Gabanna and Jean Paul Gaultier, while 15 percent prefer work by Russian designers such as Olga Komissarova, Ludmila Yakushina and Nina Donis. The good news is that 81 percent of those asked thought that Russian fashion could certainly measure up to the major Western labels.

In Canada the problem lay not so much with the powerlessness of the designers as with their lack of animo. For years, the reactions to the fashion week were mediocre, which was a direct result of the poor participation of the country's biggest names. This in turn stemmed from the lack of branding of, and funding for, local designers. With the current rise in the number of fashion weeks and particularly in the worldwide prestige of the events, the participation of Canadian designers is clearly becoming more substantial. Robin Kay, president of the Fashion Design Council Canada, feels that the country is slowly but surely gaining international recognition. Canada was previously seen as a country without a fashion identity, but that's changing. In order to be noticed internationally, the Fashion Design Council Canada put on a retrospective of the Missoni collection in Toronto in the spring of 2004. Missoni's visit to the Toronto Fashion Week would, according to Kay, strengthen Canada's position as a new player in the field of fashion. And it bore fruit, for Missoni then proposed bringing Canadian designers to Milan.

Countries where the fashion industry is still in its infancy seem to find it difficult to organise a fashion week. Such a country is Finland, where the first fashion week was organised three years ago. Despite all the efforts of the initiators, the event did not have a sequel until 2004 owing to lack of support. In the meantime, the motor behind the fashion week, trend forecaster Johanna Salovaara, has received help from various organisations within the fashion branch. There are not many fashion designers in Finland, and the ones who do operate professionally are very much locally oriented. Because of this, the Finland Fashion Week is a fairly small-scale event. In contrast to Canada, propagating Finnish couture internationally has not yet been put on the agenda. More appreciation of and publicity surrounding fashion first has to be created within Finland itself.

STRENGTHENING
Setting up fashion weeks is not always something that occurs naturally everywhere. This is only logical, seeing as fashion in many countries is still an industry in development. Of course, countries without a fashion history or identity have difficulty competing with cities like Milan or Paris that are synonymous with style. For them it is all the more important to professionalise the local infrastructure and in this way to strengthen the

position of the fashion week as a reference point in the international circuit of fashion trends.

They do this, for example, by bringing fashion out of its isolation and by expanding it with fashion-related items such as accessories, jewellery and shoes. The problem here is that it sometimes becomes difficult to distinguish between a fashion week and a traditional trade fair (think of the Collections Premieren in Düsseldorf), especially now that this formula is being applied on a grand scale. The BCN Showrooms, devoted to denim, lingerie and swimwear from national and international collections, was added to the Barcelona Fashion Week in the autumn of 2004, for example. It's a sort of 'trade zone', where commercial agents offer their wares and exchange ideas and products in a business environment. The Amsterdam Fashion Week 'District' now includes an international fashion trade fair for 'New Luxury' brands. And the Australian Fashion Week now has a similar sort of fashion fair: an exhibition space called 'The Source' that is filled with showrooms for designers and agents, a registration centre, offices for retailers and the media, a business centre, presentations of accessories, beauty products, jewellery and so on. 'For companies that have no fashion shows of their own this is an excellent way to show their products to the trendsetters who visit the shows,' says Fern Mallis, Executive Director of 7th on Sixth, the production company responsible for organising the fashion weeks in New York and Los Angeles. 'The Suites' were presented as part of the Los Angeles Fashion Week in 2004. 'We planned it in such a way that all our guests could visit the suites at "quiet" moments when there were no shows.' The goal of offering such an all-inclusive platform is two-fold: the organisation hopes to initiate fruitful collaboration between the participants as well as to serve a broad and international fashion public in the best way possible. For these reasons, Singapore adopted the formula in 2005. 'The Singapore Fashion Week will attract a congregation of who's who from the industry and redefine the parameters of sourcing and distribution for international manufacturers, fashion designers, distributors, agents, importers, retailers, garment and textile designers, merchants and international buying houses.' The Air New Zealand Fashion Week, the South African Fashion Week and the Fashion Week of the Americas employ a similar strategy. Presenting an entire lifestyle is rapidly becoming widely accepted.

PROFESSIONAL DISCOURSE
How can you further strengthen your position as a fashion country? By organising workshops and seminars that provide insight into the ins and outs of the regional fashion and textile industry and disseminate knowledge about doing business in the global market. Additional programmes are aimed at man-

ASIAN YOUNG FASHION DESIGNERS CONTEST 2004   AUSTRALIAN FASHION WEEK 2004   TORONTO FASHION WEEK 2004
                                                above: MAD CORTES
                                                under: ANNOYINGLY ENORMOUS

ufacturers, designers, buyers and other players in the field. In 2004 the Lakmé India Fashion Week initiated a series of 'Business of Fashion' seminars, and in Toronto a lecture about branding Canadian talent was held. Hong Kong presented nine seminars aimed at the industry and the market dealing with subjects such as the latest developments in the retail market for cotton garments in the United States and the influence of European environmental regulations on the textile and clothing industry. Along similar lines, the South African Fashion Week launched a two-day symposium in the summer of 2004 under the title 'The Arts and Culture Fashion Design Seminar'. An impressive list of speakers included national and international experts, such as the Milanese 'Commissioner for Fashion' Giovanni Bozzetti and a number of teachers from Central Saint Martins College of Art and Design in London. In addition, various workshops were held on a range of subjects, including:
- Developing one's own label within an existing market
- Strengthening a label with an optimal result
- Starting a business in South Africa
- The export factor
- The importance of a fashion week for a country's cultural development

The seminar was a great success and a second edition is being organised in 2005. Amsterdam, too, will be offering a lecture programme again in 2005, in addition to the catwalk shows and exhibitions. The organisation of ancillary activities mobilises and strengthens the local industry and narrows the gulf between the professional level of fashion nations and non-fashion nations, Western and non-Western countries.

SPRINGBOARD

One item of note is the increasing attention being given to newly-graduated designers, mostly by means of the introduction of awards and shows focussing on young talent. The New Star in Fashion Award is handed out at the Fashion Week of the Americas, the South African Fashion Week organises the Elle New Talent Show, Hong Kong the Young Fashion Designers Contest and the New Generation Group Collection Show is held during the Australian Fashion Week. Perhaps one of the oldest and best known is the Asian Young Fashion Designers Contest, the seventh edition of which took place in 2005. Connected with the Singapore Fashion Week, it is the only talent contest gathering promising designers from all over Asia under one heading. With representation from countries including India, Indonesia, Japan, Malaysia, Mongolia, Thailand, Sri Lanka and Vietnam, the Asian Young Fashion Designers Contest embodies the Asian potential like no other contest.

Participating in such shows is crucial for furthering the career of the young designer, who immediately builds up a lead. Becoming professional at an early stage increases their chances on the global market. 'Through my involvement in the Mercedes Australian Fashion Week I've met some of the best contacts in the industry. Thanks to my participation in the New Generation Group Collection Show my label has been seen by more than forty potential buyers, I got tremendous press coverage and managed to generate a whole lot of excitement. Right now I'm really excited because of a hefty order from Selfridges, the British department store,' declares the Australian designer Alexandra Nea. For the organisers themselves, stimulating young talent is the best way of safeguarding the future of a country's fashion industry.

ADVANCE

The size of these up and upcoming fashion weeks, the number of participants and visitors, and the professional level have grown explosively in recent years and will probably continue to do so. A few examples. The São Paulo Fashion Week is now the biggest fashion event in South America and occupies a fourth place worldwide, with a record number of around 120,000 visitors. The Russian Fashion Week has grown in three years into the biggest fashion week in Eastern Europe. The number of participants has tripled since 2002, with the result that the fashion industry in Moscow has developed in a tearing rush, growing from a few to several hundred shops. Remarkable results considering the problems at the beginning. In Amsterdam there were high expectations after the launch of the event in 2004, and after the second edition in January 2005 the initiative can now be called a great success. The number of participants, visitors and buyers has risen appreciably. Eleven official catwalk shows drew 4,000 guests and another 3,000 buyers and representatives from the press-visited 'District'. The 2005 summer edition is already in preparation. The response to the last South African Fashion Week was also overwhelming, according to Programme Director Dion Chang, which means that they are already being inundated with bookings for coming seasons.

In fact all these countries are making a head start. Here budding talent is being discovered, while in New York and Paris it is more a question of establishing names. The Western entrance of Sabyasachi Mukherjee is a good example of this, but the career path of the Brazilian designer Alexandre Herchcovitch illustrates it more than any other. He went on from the São Paulo Fashion Week to show in London and then in Paris and New York. His designs represent a unique synthesis of Brazilian and Western influences and are much in demand among clients in Brazil, the United States, Japan, Germany, China, England, Canada, Singapore, Australia and

New Zealand. These examples are not yet typical but are certainly very encouraging.

GLOBALISATION

Does all this mean that a shift is imminent in the fashion world? Or is it merely a question of a temporary trend? The question is whether all these fashion weeks are just becoming stations in the global fashion circuit. Not all initiatives are viable, of course. In my opinion the fashion weeks that last are those that build on a long textile tradition and a flourishing economy. In combination with a big sponsor, a strong market component and a supporting ancillary programme, there is a big chance of success. This explains why the fashion weeks in Singapore, China and India are so successful. The Asian fashion industry is rising fast and the United States and Europe are well aware of this. Besides the United States and Western Europe, the retail market is growing strongest in China. A country with more than a billion inhabitants that is going through an enormous economic development guarantees a major sales market. The Hong Kong Fashion Week, with 1,087 participants from sixteen countries and regions, has grown in one year by more than 11 percent. Seventy-one percent of the international buyers questioned indicated they would intensify their purchases in Asia. China still has their preference, but in its wake are South Korea, India and Taiwan. The West is feeling the pressure, certainly now that textile quotas have been abolished since 1 January 2005. One man's meat is another man's poison. New perspectives are opening for the East. 'High on the agenda at one of the seminars during the Hong Kong Fashion Week are the new challenges and opportunities as a result of the abolition of the textile quota as of 1 January 2005'. For Western fashion countries this represents a threat. Paris and Milan are already working on a joint venture to create a bigger counterweight to the East.

The threat seems to be coming mainly from the East, but the designer is becoming emancipated in South America and Africa as well. Countries like China, South Africa and Brazil no longer restrict themselves to producing for their American and European colleagues but are also concentrating on their own designs. With the help of fashion weeks, talented designers are being professionally presented and pushed in the direction of the masses. Does this mean that in the future we will be seeing a more and more integrated field? The position of Western top designers is indeed no longer unassailable. What's more, established cities like Paris and Milan are increasingly contending with the competition, and it won't be long before they lose their monopoly. In the years to come, fashion will be experienced more globally than ever before, and the worldwide advance of the fashion week is contributing to this to a large degree.

This article is largely based on Internet research. See the websites of the following fashion weeks for source material:
www.amsterdamfashionweek.com, www.mercedesbenzfashionweek.com, www.fashionweek.fi, www.fashionweek-sf.com, www.modeaparis.com, www.cameramoda.it, www.olympusfashionweek.com, www.londonfashionweek.co.uk, www.portugalfashion.com, www.spfw.ig.com.br, www.fashionweekamericas.com, www.singaporefashionweek.com, www.indiafashionweek.com, www.nzfashionweek.com, www.rfw.ru, www.reykjavikfashion.is, www.safashionweek.co.za, www.torontofashionweek.ca, www.moda-barcelona.com, www.afw.com.au, www.hkfashionweekfw.com, www.klafw.com

Sumati Nagrath

LOCAL ROOTS OF GLOBAL AMBITIONS

A look at the role of the India Fashion Week in the development of the Indian fashion industry

Over the past five years Indian designers have steadily increased their presence in the world of international fashion, especially in the ready-to-wear sector. Their small but significant steps on the international catwalk (along with those of designers from several other 'peripheral' countries) have forced us to question the validity of the 'ethnic designer' label and to re-think the categories of 'global' and 'local' fashion.[1] This essay attempts to make two distinct but related points. It first argues that while it is important to celebrate the presence of Tarun Tahiliani and Sabyasachi Mukherjee at the Milan Fashion Week in 2003 and 2004 respectively, the winning of the Designer's Choice Award at the Miami Fashion Week of the Americas by Rina Dhaka in May 2004 and the continued participation of Rajesh Pratap Singh, Kavita Bhartia and Sonal Dubal at the Singapore Fashion Week as evidence of globalisation of Indian fashion, it is equally important to ask the question: What made the globalisation of Indian fashion possible in the first place? It is important to ask this question, for it forces us to critically examine the local developments that lie at the very heart of the processes of globalisation. To present the success of Indian designer labels in stores such as Selfridges,[2] London and Lord & Taylor's,[3] New York simply as an example of the de-centring of the 'West' in the fashion hierarchy can lead to an incomplete understanding of the local processes inherently involved in the transformation of the Indian fashion industry into a global one. The second point to be made here is that while it is important to highlight the significance of 'local' developments, when it comes to fashion, local and global can no longer (if they ever were) be viewed as mutually exclusive. For while the increasing presence of non-Western countries at fashion shows and retail stores across the world is seen as challenging the very definition of global fashion, it must also be remembered that local fashion industries are themselves being moulded by their own complex interaction with the processes of globalisation .

The essay further distinguishes between the form (economic) and content (cultural) of the international fashion system. It illustrates that in the case of developing countries in general, and India particular, the national fashion industries have to adapt to what can essentially be seen as 'Western' systems/standards of production and retail if they want to be part of the global fashion industry. While the overall form of the global fashion system remains unquestioned, it is in the realm of 'content', or the creative element, that the hegemony of the West over the category of 'global' is constantly being challenged. It is in this arena the question arises: What is global fashion? It is a question that the Indian designers are responding to by doing away with the category of 'local' altogether. They argue that although they draw heavily from their Indian heritage, the clothes they create can no longer be framed in the global/local dichotomy.

OVERCOMING LOCAL IMPEDIMENTS

The recently overwhelming presence of Indian fashion on international catwalks and in high street shops across the world has been hailed as proof of the fact that fashion is now truly globalised and the West has quite literally been won. I am convinced, however, that this victory would have been quite impossible even five years ago for the simple reason that there was no Indian fashion *industry* until quite recently. In April 1998, a scathing article in one of India's leading national weekly magazines described the Indian fashion industry as 'hip, hyper and hollow' and stated that it amounted to nothing more than a 'cleverly, deliberately orchestrated hype' that was a result of the collusion between a section of the Indian media and a handful of designers (Mehra 1998). Arguing that they lacked imagination, the article criticised Indian fashion designers for restricting themselves to creating a limited selection of ornate outfits for a very small clientele rather than being about innovation, design or volumes. Aside from the unwarranted attacks on the creative talent and personal integrity of several of the designers, the article accurately drew attention to the failings of the Indian designers as entrepreneurs. It sought to highlight the fact that these designers existed at the very margins of the clothing industry with an almost negligible presence in the ready-to wear market.[4] However, what the article failed to do was to take into account the fact that the Indian fashion industry was and continues to be a relatively new entrant in the field of fashion, and despite having 'one of the oldest and richest textile histories, [its] foray into constructed clothes, as differentiated from [its] traditional draped styles, is relatively recent' (Jha 2000: 92). According to Puneet Nanda, designer for Satya Paul and director of Genesis Colors Pvt Ltd, the Indian fashion industry is still in its 'nascent stage', and that means that 'it has not really taken shape....'[5] Despite the presence of a few designers such as Ritu Kumar (one of the country's leading designers and key handicraft revivalists) since the late 1960s, the Indian fashion *industry* as such only began to take shape in the late 1980s. It was with the setting up of the country's first fashion design institute, the National Institute of Fashion Technology (NIFT),[6] in 1986 that 'fashion' as a serious 'profession' was first acknowledged . This perception was further strengthened by the setting up of high-profile couture shops such as Ensemble in 1987 and Ogaan in 1989, which housed the creations of designers such as Tarun Tahiliani, Rohit Bal and Kavita Bhartia.

However, despite these developments the Indian fashion industry continued to be denied cultural and economic legiti-

upper left: A ROHIT BAL creation for his label 'BALANCE' at the Lakme India Fashion Week, 2002
upper right: A RITU KUMAR creation from her pret à porter collection presented at Lakme India Fashion Week, 2002
under: Two SABYASACHI MUKERJEE creations from his debut showing at the Lakme India Fashion Week, 2002

macy because it remained centred on haute couture. This was especially true of the Indian wedding trousseau, which catered to a niche clientele and accounted for a majority of the profits (Mehra 1998; Taparia and Bamzai 2003). This criticism gained in strength in the early 1990s when haute couturiers in the centre of the international fashion scene began to be replaced by retailers and fashion buyers as the key arbitrators of fashion trends (Braham 1997). At this point, however, not only did the designers in India lack the basic economic and industrial infrastructure needed to create the volumes that are the bedrock of ready-to-wear lines, but the retail boom in India had yet to take off.[7] It was to address this infrastructural deficiency and to bring some sense of cohesiveness to an otherwise highly nebulous entity that the key players in the industry decided to follow the lead of countries such as USA, Britain, Canada, France and Italy[8] and set up the Fashion Design Council of India (FDCI) in December 1998. Established under the aegis of the Ministry of Textiles, the key objective of the FDCI was to foster 'the growth of the entire fashion industry in India and internationally…[to provide a] platform for designers, encourage investments and professional input in design labels [and to bolster] the growth of designer ready-to-wear lines'.[9]

LOCAL TRIUMPHS: LAKME INDIA FASHION WEEK[10]
The FDCI, realising that the only way forward for the fashion industry was to address the need to expand the industry's target customer base, opted to launch the fashion week initiative in 2000. This initiative, modelled along the lines of the fashion weeks held in New York, London, Paris and Milan, was to serve as a single platform to facilitate buyer-seller interaction within the fashion industry.[11] It would be accurate to say that since its inception, the LIFW has gone from strength to strength over the last five years. According to Tarun Tahiliani,[12] one of India's most well respected designers, the LIFW has played an 'immense role in common platforming talent, getting unprecedented amounts of press [coverage] and creating an organised market week that buyers can congregate to.' The importance of bringing buyers and sellers face to face has translated into both international and national successes for the Indian fashion industry. While on the international front it has led to an increased presence of Indian designers at events such as Selfridges' Bollywood promotion, nationally it has meant the creation and fostering of strategic partnerships between designers and retailer. An excellent example of the evolving strategic partnerships between the designers and the corporate sector is the establishment of the designer retail outlet, Be:. Owned by the Indian conglomerate Raymond Ltd,[13] Be: is India's first multi-brand designer ready-to-wear retail outlet, now expanded to fourteen outlets since it opened its first store in New Delhi in

July 2001. A partnership such as this works to the benefit of the retailer, the designer and the consumer. While the retailer gets to determine the price points, standardise sizes and forecast trends, the designers have access to an assured market and the consumers can finally buy designer wear at affordable prices. As Goa-based designer Wendell Rodricks points out,[14] 'LIFW has been the best thing to happen to modern Indian fashion. It has brought order, organisation, schedule, commerce and knowledge to both professionals and the Indian public at large.' It has helped overcome the 'the disorganised state of affairs [and] lack of support' that, according to Rodricks, formed a major obstacle in the Indian fashion industry's attempt to go global. The success of the LIFW in transforming the prevailing perceptions of the Indian fashion industry nationally is also apparent in the fact that by its fifth outing, the magazine that had earlier dismissed it as 'hip, hyper and hollow' in September 2004, carried a cover story on India's top ten designers. In a complete reversal of opinion it now argued that the Indian fashion industry was not being taken seriously enough in the country and that some of the designers were not just 'worthy heirs' to India's heritage of costume and embellishment but were highly creative people with a strong business sense (Dhar 2004).

While acknowledging the success of the LIFW in helping to establish the legitimacy of the Indian fashion industry as a viable economic entity nationally, it is important to note that the LIFW, both in its inspiration and its structure, is essentially a creation of the 'Western' fashion system and carries within it a certain institutional logic. Since the Indian fashion industry is a relatively new entrant on the global fashion scene, it has meant that in order to participate in it, the 'local' industry has perforce had to operate within a pre-existing system. This is evidenced by the fact that one of the highlights of the third LIFW was the launch of a trend book,[15] the explicit aim of which is to help the Indian fashion design industry adopt the 'efficient' system predicated on elements of the Western fashion world such as the cycle of season (Nagrath 2003). Further proof of the fact that all 'local' industries must work within a single global system can be seen in the advancing of the dates of LIFW 2004 from July to April. This decision was taken by the FDCI to ensure that the LIFW is in tandem with the international buying season, enabling international buyers to place their orders well in time to meet their requirements for the fall/winter season abroad. It is not the existence of a single global fashion system, but the fact that some centres (mainly located in the West) continue to set the industrial parameters of this system, that is problematic, for it confirms India's 'subordinate status as a late developer, forcibly compelled to modernise in Western terms [....] Competition is still on someone else's ground, within an idiom and a tradi-

A SATYA PAUL creation for his pret label 'U' at the Lakme India Fashion Week 2002

tional developed elsewhere' (Kondo 1997: 56). While buckling under the homogenising forces of the industrial structures of the global fashion system, we find Indian designers simultaneously challenging the Orientalist notions that seek to describe them as 'inadequate imitators of Western fashion' (Kondo 1997: 68) and rejecting the global/local divide through their designs.

DEFYING CATEGORISATION: DESIGNERS SPEAK UP
Writing in the New York Times, well-known author Shashi Tharoor said, 'As an Indian writer living in New York, I find myself constantly asked a question with which my American confreres never have to contend: "But whom do you write for?"' (Tharoor 2001). This is also a question faced by any Indians designer who seeks to reach an audience beyond the territorial boundaries of India or its extensive diaspora. Inherent in the question is the assumption that there exist at least two mutually exclusive target audiences – the local and the global – and to cater to one means abandoning the other. Rodricks[16] articulates the voice of the Indian fashion fraternity when he says, 'There is no such difference for me.' He goes on to add: 'I believe that the world can wear contemporary Indian clothes anywhere. Why should we follow the West? Ideally, my clothes combine Indian roots with international wearability.' This idea of combining Indian sensibilities with international wearability finds resonance with Ritu Kumar,[17] who says, 'I use a lot of local crafts in my work, but it does not necessarily look or mean that it needs an indigenous inspiration – it can look global but hand crafted.' Tahiliani on the other hand, while distinguishing between his Indian and 'Western' clothing lines, argues that they are both equally wearable in the local and the global context. He says, 'As a modern Indian, I am comfortable equally with the genre I have created in both. I am Indian but dream in English. My Western clothing is full of Indianness – in colour, shapes and various visual or style references. Likewise, my most classic bridals may be corseted to give a better shape (this being an entirely Western notion). There is no conflict. I am what I am to both worlds. They both exist in India so I am not consciously doing something for the Western world.'[18] What becomes increasingly clear from the statements made by the designers is that 'Indian' fashion, like any other cultural product of a postcolonial nation, is 'inevitably hybridised involving a dialectical relationship between European ontology and epistemology and the impulse to create or re-create independent local identity' (Ashcroft et al. 1995: 95). Defying the dichotomies such as local/global, Western/Oriental, traditional/modern, the work of Indian fashion designers compels us to re-think the definition of fashion itself.

A SATYA PAUL creation for his pret label 'U' at the Lakme India Fashion Week 2002

NOTES

[1] The term 'ethnic' is a loaded one that has serious political, social and cultural implications, as the labelling of a group of people as such implies that they lie outside the mainstream and carries with it an element of marginalisation. (Ashcroft et al., 1998, pp. 81-82) The fact that both the designs and designers from India are not yet completely free of the rather problematic label of 'ethnic' was brought home at an international conference on fashion, 'Making an Appearance', held at the University of Queensland, Australia, in July 2003. Speaking in a panel entitled 'Meet the Designers', Pam Easton and Lydia Pearson of the Easton Pearson label pointed out that one of the hurdles they faced while establishing their brand was the need to 'demystify' the idea that since some of their work was based in India they were an 'ethnic' brand. They realised that their perception as an ethnic brand would mean they would remain restricted to a niche market and never be able to break into the mass market. So they had to tell people that the clothes didn't originate from India and didn't even look Indian. They simply used the skills of craftspeople in India and not their designs.

[2] In May 2002 one of London's biggest department stores chose to showcase a number of Indian designers during its special 'Bollywood' theme promotion.

[3] In May 2003 Lord & Taylor's flagship store on 5th Avenue, Manhattan, showcased an 'Into India' theme and the four designers featured were Rina Dhaka, Vivek Narang, Manish Arora and Tarun Tahiliani.

[4] In 2001-02 the domestic designer wear industry accounted for only 2 percent of India's total branded apparel market, which in turn is only a fraction of total consumer spending in India. (Taparia and Bamzai, 2003)

[5] E-mail Interview with the author, December 2004.

[6] The National Institute of Fashion Technology was set up in1986 under the aegis of the Indian government's Ministry of Textiles to foster fashion business education in the country. It now has branches in seven cities in India: New Delhi, Bangalore, Chennai, Gandhinagar, Hyderabad, Kolkata and Mumbai.

[7] The boom in the organised retail industry in India took place in the late 1990s and continues to grow today with the opening up of malls and hypermarts all across the country's urban landscape. This development in the retail industry is seen as a consequence of the deregulation and liberalisation of the Indian economy in 1991.

[8] Fashion design councils and associations in most countries were set up to provide support and create cohesiveness in the fashion industries in their respective countries/cities.

[9] FDCI promotional material.

[10] Lakme has been the main sponsor of the India Fashion Week since its very inception, hence the name Lakme India Fashion Week.

[11] The LIFW website http://www.lakmeindiafashionweek.com/background.htm) describes the idea behind a fashion week this way: unlike individual 'couture' fashion shows, which showcase a one-of-a-kind designer collection, the focus of a 'fashion week' is more trade-oriented, where the clothes showcased are representative samples that can then be produced in larger quantities and various sizes for sale through multiple outlets. Hence, the event takes on a more 'serious business' orientation as compared with the more 'dramatic/theatrical/social' slant of couture shows.

[12] E-mail interview with author, December 2004.

[13] Raymond is a 1.4-billion rupee conglomerate, with industries that include cement, yarn and steel. But the group has refocused on textiles and ready-mades.

[14] E-mail interview with author, December 2004.

[15] The trend book was released by Promostyl, a Paris-based trend and design bureau.

[16] E-mail interview with author, December 2004

[17] E-mail interview with author, December 2004

[18] E-mail interview with author, December 2004

REFERENCES:

Ashcroft B., G. Griffiths, H. Tiffin, eds. – THE POST COLONIAL READER – London: Routledge, 1995.

Ashcroft, B., G. Griffiths and H. Tiffin – H. KEY CONCEPTS IN POST-COLONIAL STUDIES – New York: Routledge, 1998.

Braham, P – 'Fashion: Unpacking a Cultural Production', in: PRODUCTION OF CULTURE, CULTURE OF PRODUCTION – ed. P. Du Gay. London: Sage, 1997.

Dhar, Shobita – 'Birds of Plume' – OUTLOOK, 20 September 2004.

Jha, Banhi – INDIAN FASHION: THIS DECADE AND THE NEXT, EVOLVING TRENDS IN FASHION, THE NIFT MILLENNIUM DOCUMENT 2000 – NIFT Publication Division: Delhi, 2000.

Kondo, Dorinne – ABOUT FACE: PERFORMING RACE IN FASHION AND THEATRE – London: Routledge, 1997.

Mehra, Sunil – 'Hip, Hyper Hollow', OUTLOOK – 20 April 1997.

Nagrath, S – '(En)countering Orientalism in High Fashion: A review of India Fashion Week 2002', FASHION THEORY 7, 3-4 (2003): 361-376. –

Taparia, Nidhi and Kaveree Bamzai – 'What's Hot What's Not', INDIA TODAY – 21 July 2003, 60-65.

Tharoor, Shashi – 'Expanding Boundaries With a Colonial Legacy', THE NEW YORK TIMES, 30 July 2001 –

EXPLORING CULTURAL HERITAGE IN A GLOBAL WORLD?

Through the growing popularity of Fashion Weeks and the possibilities of internet it is fast becoming easier for small scale, local fashion labels to reach a global public. In this category we find labels and designers who, in the first instance, develop their abilities in their own culture and then seek entry into the international fashion market. Their motives are often idealistic: they endeavour to retain their own culture and deliberately and consciously attempt to find employment for craftsmen from their own countries, whom they pay well.

PINEDA COVALIN

Pineda Covalin was founded in 1996 by two young Mexican designers, Christina Pineda (born in 1977) and Ricardo Covalin (born in 1978). They find their inspiration in pre-Hispanic Mexican culture and are trying to keep traditional Mexican ceremonies, customs and myths alive. Pineda and Covalin became acquainted in the summer of 1994 in Merida, Yucatan, where they were both taking part in a project devoted to preserving the local culture.

'To get to know the people and the area, we visited archaeological sites, ruins and colonial areas and lived in the indigenous communities. Many of the community members were unemployed artists, and we taught them how to make original designs in various colours, shapes and sizes and to sell them as a way to support their families. We fell in love with pre-Hispanic culture,' says Covalin.

www.pinedacovalin.com

After completing her textile studies at the University of Mexico City, Pineda was asked to design a product for the shop attached to the Museum of Anthropology in Mexico City. In collaboration with Ricardo Covalin she designed a number of ties and shawls in the spirit of the things they brought with them from Yucatan. They found a company that wanted to produce their designs, but only if the minimum order was 10,000 pieces. The museum was unable to finance this and so they decided to do the work of realising the designs themselves. Initially the two designers had to go from shop to shop with a full suitcase in an attempt to sell their wares, but since then Pineda Covalin has grown into a flourishing business with a steadily rising turnover.

Their success is partly due to the dominant trend in Mexican society to choose home-grown rather than foreign products. At the same time, the silk ties, bags, cushions and jewellery with designs and symbols from Mayan and Aztec culture are selling well abroad, especially in museum shops and exclusive boutiques. It goes without saying that their work is also being shown during the Mexican Fashion Week. MF

PINEDA COVALIN, accessory line 2005

SUN GODD'ESS

'Sun Godd'ess African Couture is a celebration and a reflection of the cultures we were born into. Our designs are greatly inspired by the original designs worn by the people of South Africa in days gone by. The appeal of our clothes also lies in the lovely and exciting design combinations of modern fabrics and embellishments, with a good dose of pure nostalgia. In fact each designing session is like a trip in which we retell the rich African folktales from childhood, so in the end our clothes not only celebrate where we come from, but they also open up new perspectives for the future. We believe that the nostalgic designs of our clothes express a particular lifestyle we all seek to enjoy.'

This is how the husband and wife team of Thando and Vanya Mangaliso describe their Sun Godd'ess label, established in 2001. The name and the

logo were derived from the book Indaba My Children by the African artist Credo Mutw, which depicts the love and pride that Africans have for their country. Thando and Vanya Mangaliso also have the same intention. They take original South African designs as their starting point and translate them into today's styles, creating colourful, decorated outfits inspired by traditional South African clothing such as skirts and bustiers embellished with a Venda print, Tswana cotton shirts and a series of richly decorated bags and belts inlaid with beads. The husband and wife team work closely with Sicelo Ntshalintshali and local designers who, like them, take traditional African garments as a source of inspiration. The appeal of Sun Godd'ess lies in the unique combination of modern fabrics and a measure of African history. At the moment Sun Godd'ess is one of

South Africa's most successful fashion houses. The label has three shops in South Africa and is gradually conquering a market in Asia. AS

www.sungoddess.co.za

SUN GODD'ESS, a/w 2003/2004

LAM DE WOLF

'Sinnerokken' refers to the chambers of rhetoric, the literary guilds from the fifteenth and sixteenth centuries that promoted the writing of lyrics and especially morality plays ('sinnespelen').

Sinnerokken are skirts that propagate an idea or a moral. De Wolf's skirts are constructed from traditional and modern fabrics onto which she has embroidered texts by writers, artists and others. Each skirt is in the form of a long tube which can be worn on both sides. If you want to announce the text, you wear the skirt embroidered side out, but if you want to keep the message to yourself then you wear it on the inside.

Lam de Wolf (born in Badhoevedorp, 1949) has been working on her Sinnerokken since 2004. She saves texts from books, newspapers and television that deal with living a conscious life, injustice, mortality and insight. De Wolf studied 'monumental textiles' at the Gerrit Rietveld Academy. In the eighties she was mainly known for her jewellery designs which sometimes looked more like items of clothing or pieces of art. Much of her early work is to be found in Dutch museums. De Wolf exhibits regularly in galleries and museums at home and abroad. In 1984 she received an honourable mention at the Textile Biennial in Vichte, Belgium. MF

SINNEROK, 2004
collection Centraal Museum
Sinnerok with the text 'Stilte' [Silence] by Remco Campert

SINNEROK, 2004
collection Centraal Museum
Sinnerok with a quotation from Jacques Brel's 'The passion and the pain'.

WETEN
HET ER IS.
OP EEN BESCHEIDEN,
DE TELEFOON OP EN
WOORD
BEWEEGT EN
WEG, ALS JE

DENE FUR CLOUDS

'Have you any idea how wonderful it feels to be in Paris and Montreal and see our designs and garments on the catwalk, knowing they were made by our group in Fort Providence. We have succeeded in making an impact both in our own community and in the international fashion market. Our collection actually appeared in three European fashion magazines! For thousands of years, indigenous people around the world have used the natural resources of their local environments in an ecologically sustainable manner, and Dene Fur Clouds is continuing that tradition.'

So says Nellie Norwegian, one of the women behind Dene Fur Clouds, a company that has been run by a group of eleven Indians from Fort Providence in the Canadian Northwest Territories since 1997. The tribe is called Dene – 'de' means stream and 'ne' Mother Earth. The ten women in the group are

www.ek-o.net

joined by a man who carves the buttons and other decorations out of antlers. The company was idle for a year in 2000, but was able to resume activities in 2001 after being taken over by the Northwest Territories Development Corporation. The ancestors of these Indians made 'fur clouds', blankets and lightweight garments of strips of rabbit and beaver fur which they combined with wool and finger-knitted together. Dene Fur Clouds have adapted and modernised these traditional techniques and designs and now use them to produce contemporary fashion items and interior accessories.

The fashion line is called E'ko, which means 'Look out!', and consists of knitted winter accessories made of fur such as hats, scarves and gloves, as well as sweaters, vests, legwarmers, cushions and blankets. Geometrical patterns from traditional hunting

clothes can be seen in all the designs. The Dene work the way they always have: self-sufficiently and in a way that is ecologically sound. They use the skins of the animals they eat and throw nothing away.

The 2003/2004 collection was shown in Paris under the auspices of a promotion campaign for Furworks International and appeared in several European fashion magazines. Apart from Paris, Dene Fur Clouds also presented itself at the Toronto Fashion Week. Both the garments and the interior accessories are for sale. Everything is washable.

DENE FUR CLOUDS, Ek'o, s/s 2003/2004

detail, DENE FUR CLOUDS, E'ko 2003/2004

Detail, DENE FUR CLOUDS, Ek'o, s/s 2003/2004

RITU KUMAR

In the late 1960s India was going through profound changes. Plastics had replaced mud, brass and silver, factory-produced papers and woods took the place of sophisticated handicrafts and nylons displaced an ancient heritage of cotton and silk. It was not only a battle between tradition and modernity; it was also a confrontation of lifestyles and values. During this time, a small group who had benefited from unique opportunities of study and travel began to see the depth of the craft and design heritage of their own country. They discovered that India was a reservoir of delicate skills.

In an attempt to merge their international experiences with the skills of Indian people, they came to the conclusion that contemporary designers must revitalise their own roots and identities. This was essential if Indian creativity was to be taken out into the world in a way that benefited both craftsmen and the modern consumer. This scattered group, including Ritu Kumar (Amritsar India, 1944), were to become the country's leading designers of buildings, garments, fabric and accessories. Kumar studied Western art history and museology before starting as a fashion designer with hand block printers and two tables in a small village near Calcutta. In the last 28 years, Kumar's team of dedicated workers has progressed to produce some of the country's most exquisite garments and accessories in cotton, silk and leather. These embrace both traditional textile crafts and the lineage of Indian design. Traditional skills that had been lost over the centuries have been revitalised, and this has enabled the craftsmen to continue working in their own environment. Kumar has pioneered the term 'fashion' in the Indian context, and more importantly has demonstrated that hand-made products can be as profitable and even more glamorous than those made by machine.

Ritu Kumar's forte is traditional Indian clothes that draw heavily on the textile and embroidery heritage of India and remain classics of their kind. But she has evolved another style for the European buyer. Her Indo-Western fusion wear combines block prints, embroidery and craft inputs with a Western style.

Ritu Kumar has stores throughout India. She has designed wardrobes for three Miss Indias, comprising swimwear, evening wear, traditional Indian wear, casual wear and formal evening gowns. AS

www.ritukumar.com

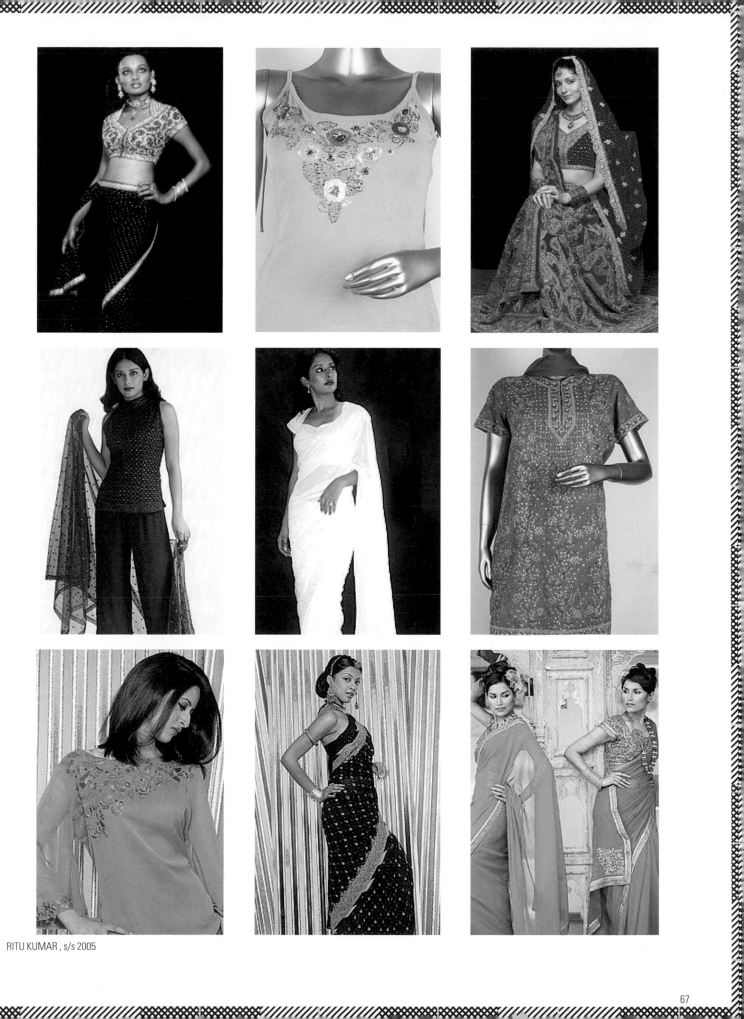

RITU KUMAR , s/s 2005

RAZU MIKHINA

Razu Mikhina is an internationally acclaimed Russian design company that creates fabric prints and women's wear. Its designer, Daria Razumikhina, trained at Central St Martins, London (1995-1998) and launched her own label in 1999.

Daria is Russian and was born in Moscow. She studied at Moscow State University and has a PhD in linguistics. She worked as an interpreter and journalist for foreign TV channels and newspapers before going to London to study fashion design. She was admitted to Central St Martins to study fashion print. After returning to Russia in 1998 she created her own label, Razu Mikhina, her surname split in two. Her first show was held in Moscow in January 1999. Daria stages all her shows in Moscow.

Razu Mikhina's collections mix different shapes, colours and moods, creating an eclectic urban style. Oriental influences are merged with traditional Russian ornaments. Russian lace, still handmade by old ladies in the northern town of Vologda, ribbons and braid used in traditional Russian costumes, and Russian felt and linen are all combined in contemporary proportions to create a sophisticated, exotic, postfolk look.

All fabrics, materials, trimmings and clothes are produced and manufactured in Russia. Her latest collection showcases the trademark Razu Mikhina lace and ribbon skirts, coats and jackets as well as hand-embroidered ornamental and appliquéd garments, all creating a romantic, somewhat folkloric, feminine look for next season.

'My clothes are for intelligent, sophisticated women from everywhere who want something different and strongly individual,' says the designer, Daria Razumikhina.

,

www.razumikhina.com

RAZU MIKHINA, May 2004

CHINA LANE

'In order to understand the essence of traditional embroidery I took a trip to Gui-zhou and stayed with the Miao tribe for two weeks last year. The whole trip turned out to be very memorable. Not only was I impressed by the amazing scenery, but also by the sincere and colourful local customs, unique folk culture and historic heritage. It's very interesting to find out how diversified and detailed the hand-embroidered stitches can be from one Miao tribe to another.

'"I learned embroidery at four years of age from my mum. It's a heritage for us to do embroidery. We have been doing it all of our lives. We hand-embroider our clothes, our blankets, our shoes…", my 52-year-old Miao embroidery teacher told me. In the past, embroidery was one of the key factors in making a good marriage: a girl was able to marry a better husband and into a better family if her embroidery work was good. Nowadays, however, with the modernisation of society, the new generation of Miao girls don't learn traditional embroidery techniques anymore. They often go to the city and find jobs as office girls or waitresses, because doing embroidery can't earn them any serious money. Result: they have lost interest in doing this heavy and time-consuming craftwork.

While I was overwhelmed by their amazing embroidery work, I felt sad to see the loss of those traditional hand-stitches and crafts . After I returned home from Gui-zhou, I decided to promote hand embroidery by incorporating the stitches into the China Lane collection. I hope that through China Lane's international sales and distribution, people will get to appreciate the beauty and delicacy of hand embroidery once more. In return, this will help the girls of the Miao tribe earn their living with their traditional handwork and to promote the local economy. This way the tradition will be able to carry on and will be preserved for the coming generations.'

Shirley Cheung Laam (born in Fujian, China, 1974) emigrated at the age of ten from China to Hong Kong. She studied economics at the University of Chicago and afterwards attended the Parsons School of Design in New York. After a brief career as a fashion buyer she started China Lane in 2002 with a small collection of loungewear and lingerie made of pure silk and pashmina cashmere embellished with hand-embroidered Chinese motifs. She has designed her first prêt-à-porter collection for the winter of 2005/2006, which is on sale at the Paris fair. AS

CHINA LANE, detail 2005/2006

www.china-lane.com

detail CHINA LANE, a/w 2005/2006

detail CHINA LANE, a/w 2005/2006

MANISH ARORA

On graduating from the National Institute of Fashion Technology in 1994, Manish Arora (born in India, 1974) received the prize for the most creative student of the year and since then has been active as a fashion designer. He settled in New Delhi and soon became one of the top Indian fashion designers. In 1994 he won second prize in the Smirnoff Fashion Awards and in 1995 was second in the Young Asians Designers Competition, in which he also won the prize for the most original collection. The French Vogue company immediately offered him a job, but Arora decided to stay in India and to start his own label: 'Manish Arora'. A ready-to-wear ladies' collection, 'Fishfry', followed in February 2001. In addition to developing his labels, Manish works as a stylist for various Indian magazines.

Manish Arora thinks that fashion should be rooted in local culture but at the same time should be international and fulfil international taste criteria. In Arora's case this is translated into collections in which bright, typically Indian colours and parodies of Indian popular culture are combined with clothing that, in terms of silhouette and form, adheres to international fashion trends. The result is a mix of Indian details and youthful clothes in accordance with the latest international trends in fashion.

In 2004 Arora was invited by the exclusive Parisian shop Maria Luisa to present his summer collection alongside labels like John Galliano and Alexander McQueen. So for leading Indian designer Manish Arora a place at the top of the international fashion scene no longer seems far away. MF

Rocinha Seamstress and Craftwork Cooperative Ltd, or Coopa Roca for short, is a cooperative of 150 women from Rocinha, one of the biggest slum districts in Brazil. The women of Coopa Roca are trying to preserve traditional Brazilian handicrafts and to use them to support themselves. In this way they can continue to work at home and at the same time care for their children. Maria Theresa Leal, the organisation's head, takes care of commissions, external communications and, if necessary, the nursery. All decisions are taken collectively at the office in the centre of the Favela.

www.rediff.com

MANISH ARORA, s/s 2005

MANISH ARORA,
n/w 2003/2004

76

COOPA ROCA

Leal started Coopa Roca in 1981 after having done a waste textile recycling project with children from Rocinha. She discovered that the women from the region, the Nordestinas, were very good at sewing quilts and cushions for the local market. Leal saw the commercial and fashion potential of their craftsmanship, which could improve the social status of the Rocinha community. In the meantime Coopa Roca has grown into an international brand that supplies handiwork techniques to a number of well-known Brazilian designers such as Carlos Miele, as well as to C&A South America and the artist Tord Boontje. Recently, Coopa Roca even started its own clothing line which is being shown at the São Paolo Fashion Week.

Coopa Roca works mainly with waste material from local textile manufacturers, using such traditional techniques as drawstring appliqué, crocheting and macramé. The collection is colourful and based on Brazil's multifaceted culture. AS

www.ashoka.org

COOPA ROCA, dress, 1994

COOPA ROCA, dress, 200

COOPA ROOCA, s/s 2005

Ted Polhemus

WHAT TO WEAR IN THE GLOBAL VILLAGE?

Surely even that great visionary Marshal McLuhan could not have foreseen the extent to which his 1962 prediction of 'the Global Village' would become a reality. More even than the merging and interfacing of the world's mass media (the beginnings of which McLuhan observed in his lifetime), the World Wide Web has collapsed and obliterated geography itself. To demonstrate this one need only go to a search engine like Google, type in 'global+village' and come up with 2,910,000 hits. The telling point being that you can do this anywhere on the planet and, additionally, that wherever you conduct such a search you will be getting results which *themselves* originated anywhere on the planet. Indeed, cruising through the Internet ether we are often actually oblivious to place. Physical geography has become irrelevant and often unknowable – just as McLuhan predicted.

At the same time as the electronic mass media and the World Wide Web have hot-wired the planet into one single communication network, the inexorable advance of globalisation has implanted the same Western institutions, culture, attitudes, ideas and branded products into every corner and crevice of the planet. Today someone in Moscow, someone in Buenos Aires, someone in Sydney and someone in Bangalore can all eat the same meal in the same fast food restaurant, drive the same car, watch the same movie, struggle with the same computer software, drink the same beer, lust after the same pop star and wear the same clothes, shoes and watch. In this sense, not only is the world interconnected, it is culturally continuous, amalgamated, united.

Yet remarkably, despite all this, the world persists in its diversity and particularity – indeed, in a very real sense the significance of the local has, if anything, become greater. In countless old science fiction movies, whenever the crew of the spaceship contacts earth on the video phone, earth (and any other planet) is inevitably depicted as a culturally homogeneous whole governed by a sensible 'Federation' within which everyone is a citizen of the world, the implication being that in the distant future we would have the sense to put aside archaic local differences and blend seamlessly into one uniform, undifferentiated global entity. It is this sense of a global village – of globalisation as a lowest common denominator of sameness, of international conformity brought on by a withering away of local/national differences – which (together with the view that in the future everyone would dress identically) the science fiction writers got completely wrong.

Perhaps in reaction to this onslaught of globalisation, regional and national identities are now cherished as never before. This is especially evident in 'the West',[1] where we crave sushi from Japan, batik prints from Java, kung fu movies from Hong Kong, tango from Argentina, beaded jewellery from East Africa, etc. precisely for their cultural otherness, the fact that they have not been ground down and obliterated by the seemingly unstoppable advance of the glaciers of globalisation. Accordingly, like a new breed of pilgrims, we travel in ever greater numbers over ever greater distances in pursuit of ways of life other than our own. And while we hope the rest of the world will continue to buy 'our' products for the sake of 'our' economies and 'our' jobs, we also desperately hope that somehow (surely against all odds) these other places will retain their exotic cultural distinctiveness.

Nor is this persistence of the local simply a matter of 'us' versus 'them', a continuation of the West's long love affair with the exotic. Even *within* the West we have not seen the withering away of national or regional differences to form a single monolithic culture, as once seemed inevitable. Quite the opposite, in fact. For example, however far the European Union may move toward political and economic merger, national and even tiny regional identities not only continue to exist within Europe, but they thrive – if only in the popular imagination.

Such national identities are rarely if ever objective social facts. They are mythologies, fictions which immediately appear ridiculous when articulated (as will be all too evident in this essay), yet they nevertheless retain enormous power, even over those of us who like to think of ourselves as too rational and/or too politically correct to entertain crude stereotypes. Consider: A Dutch woman goes on holiday to Italy and during the course of this holiday she meets an Italian man. Maybe the Dutch woman (possibly because she's seen a lot of films featuring Marcelo Mastroianni) is thinking that all Italian men are romantic and great lovers. Maybe the Italian man (having heard that Holland is an extremely liberal country) is thinking that all Dutch women are 'easy' and (coming from a country too coolly rational, like all of northern Europe) highly susceptible to Latin passions. Maybe they are about to discover just how wrong national stereotypes can be. Or could this turn out to be a self-fulfilling prophecy?

However much we believe ourselves to be immune to such clearly unverifiable and often downright absurd national or regional stereotypes, the fact is that it is virtually impossible to insulate ourselves from their influence. These are ridiculous clichés which most of us reject on a conscious, articulate level but which, bubbling away under the surface, continue to shape our lives. Open a map of the world, close your eyes and let your finger come to rest on any country in the world. Whatever country it is, it immediately triggers unsubstantiated yet powerful adjectives: boring, sexy, dangerous, efficient, chaotic, lazy, dirty,[2] passionate, extroverted, serious, strange,

upper left: FEMALE WEAVER, Peru

lower left: BRAZILIAN CARNAVAL, Rio de Janeiro, photo: Guy Moberly

upper right: strung beated jewellery of the MASAI, Afrika

lower right: DANCERS, Hawaii

inhibited, casual, cool, chic, naff and so forth and so on. While most of us would think twice about voicing such absurd stereotypes, if we are honest we must acknowledge that they lurk there under the surface and that they influence our actions more than we would care to admit. The world, in other words, has not become a continuous, undifferentiated, homogenous whole. Place continues to convey meaning and such meanings – however clichéd, stereotyped, fanciful and unsubstantiated – continue to motivate us; influencing our consumer choices (with, as we will see, particular relevance to fashion design).

Even if we don't actually succumb to the holiday romance with someone from another country (and how many of us, hand on heart, can say that we have never at least entertained such fantasies?), surely our choice of holiday destination is more often than not motivated by a perception of that country or region which wouldn't hold up under objective scrutiny. Now one of the world's largest industries, tourism is founded upon the belief that, despite globalisation, cultural diversity persists, and more often than not it is motivated by a search for particular configurations of otherness which address something missing in ourselves and our own way of life. We travel to a particular country with particular mythical expectations of what we will find. Of course, like our hypothetical couple above, such an experience may serve to swiftly demolish any such ill-founded expectations, but – given that any sensible country wishing to maintain its tourist industry will do its best to transform itself into a sort of theme park of its mythologised self, and given that the tourist also has a vested interest in finding what s/he hoped to find – actual travel may ironically have the effect of further reinforcing even the most logically flimsy of national stereotypes.

Countries are brands and, as such, they experience shifts in their perception and popularity; they move in and out of fashion. A succinct history of the fashions of geography over the last forty-two years is exemplified by the James Bond movies. Each year our hero – the ultimate tourist – travels to that country (Japan, Brazil, Russia, Italy, Thailand, etc.) that is beginning to register on the most avant-garde radar apparatus as the sort of 'in' location that a plugged-in, sophisticated, man/woman of the world would want to visit. However unrealistic, stereotyped and fantastic (there are presumably women in Brazil who do not wear tiny g-strings, men in Argentina who are not macho cowboys, football players or tango dancers, people in Holland who do not smoke marijuana, Russians who do not drink vast quantities of vodka, Australians who don't surf, Italians who are not great lovers, etc.), such national brands have enormous power in the world today with profound political and economic impact. Obviously, the perception of each national brand will dramatically affect that country's tourism,

but this is only one component of the way these national brands (clearly the most influential marketing constructs in the world today) influence all aspects of consumer choice. For example, Brand Germany (lacking in humour but serious and technically rigorous) is good for BMW while Brand Ireland (convivial, friendly, traditional, erudite) is good for Guinness. Other than tourism, however, no industry is as interlinked with national branding as fashion is.

Throughout its history, fashion has surveyed the world for style ideas, transforming traditional designs and textiles into the latest new look. Increasingly, however, it is the significance, the underlying meaning (even if, in truth, it is of our own invention) rather than the aesthetics of traditional garments, textiles or accessories that particularly attracts us. We value the generic signification 'Not globalised' that naturally attaches to all such items. And garments or accessories that derive from a particular region or nationality tap into the brand message of that place. Essentially narratives about alternative ways of life, regional/national brands are particularly desirable in contemporary fashion, which is increasingly becoming focused on the articulation of alternative ways of life in the form of 'lifestyle'. Briefly put, both regional/national brands and fashion are ethnographic sketches, projections of alternative, hypothetical ways of life, and as such they have a logical affinity. While geographic brands are symbolically visualised by means of national costume (the sari of India, the tanga of Brazil), fashion regularly stitches regional/national brand narratives into the semiotic fabric of its own utopian visions.

To properly understand the how and the why of the increasingly intimate (and passionate) relationship between Other Places and the clothing, accessory and beauty industries requires that we briefly explore some of the relevant characteristics of fashion today – characteristics that facilitate and motivate this relationship in a way which would not have occurred previously. Profound changes that have taken place in the last fifty years have rendered fashion almost unrecognisable in comparison to what it was in previous eras – changes not only in the look of garments but, more significantly, in the fashion system itself.[3] We will return to consider other aspects of this transformation in the later part of this essay, but for now, to appreciate why fashion is particularly drawn to regional/national branding, it is important to note the extent to which appearance has become 'statement' – a semiological rather than simply an aesthetic phenomenon – and the underlying reasons for this shift in function.[4] As is always the case, this shift in our approach to our presentations of self reveals equally profound shifts in our social fabric.[5] A key problem of our time (indeed, one which arguably defines our postmodern era) is that of socio-cultural identity – and the

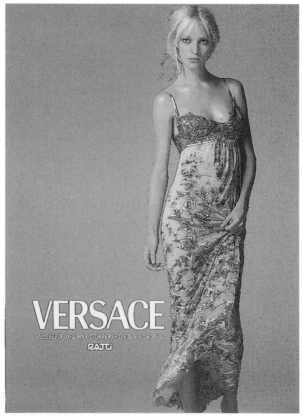

upper left: MEN IN KILTS, Scotland
lower left: VERSACE, advertising campaign, 1997

lower right: DIESEL, advertising campaign 'THE FUTURE. A MUSICAL TO BELIEVE IN', s/s 2005

articulation of that identity. Until quite recent times 'People Like Us' were readily and verbally classifiable according to the established socio-cultural criteria of class, religion, race, ethnic background, etc. Today, however, while such traditional socio-cultural classifiers still exist, they no longer prove adequate in describing, characterising and classifying identity. We are no longer bound by these conditions of our birth, and our true identities today are rooted in less easily articulated differences in attitude, vision, philosophy, desire and dreams – what people in marketing have labelled 'lifestyle'.

At the heart of lifestyle is style – today's vital, indispensable language of identity. From an ever-growing supermarket of style (where every object from our kitchen to our watch, our dinner to our trousers, our car to our mobile phone is available in a previously unimaginable design range) we choose those items which signify most precisely where we are 'at'. (Or, given the fact that such personal advertising is no more accurate and honest than any other form of advertising, we choose those items which signify most precisely where we would like others to *believe* we are 'at'.) In this process of exploring and explaining ourselves visually, objects which might once have been purchased simply because they 'look nice' are now chosen because they 'say' the right things or make the most effective translation of those values, beliefs, dreams, desires and so forth which we hold dear and consider to be core components of our identity. While this is true of all types of consumer objects (and goes a long way to explaining our age's preoccupation with design in all forms), those objects which make up our presentation of self are especially important in this regard because they are portable (you can't take your new kitchen with you to a night-club) and personal (the link between self and appearance seen as uniquely immediate, intimate and requiring special commitment).

Fashion statements can employ two separate and distinctive systems of signification. Firstly, there is the semiotics of style itself (colour, cut, pattern, material, geographic or historical reference, etc.) and, secondly, there is the semiotics of brands where the lifestyle vision of a particular brand/designer is compressed into and released through that brand/designer's logo and overall marketing presence. In the first instance, if I wear, for example, a black beret, then certain significations (artistic, nonconformist, Beat, Parisian, early twentieth-century, Bohemian, etc.) may be read into this 'adjective'. In the second instance, if, say, I wear a jumper with a Benetton logo, then those lifestyle concepts which Benetton has cultivated in its past and present advertising campaigns (roughly put: anti-racism, social and environmental responsibility, but also, increasingly, the implication that such social concerns are compatible with the pursuit of pleasure and the good life

within the context of a united, global culture) becomes part of the subtext of my own style statement.

Any effective, successful brand projects its own mythical sense of place/geography – a virtual, utopian theme park where its particular matrix of desire, belief and dreams (life as it could be/should be lived) can be perfectly realised. VersaceLand, DieselLand, DiorLand, GaultierLand, RalphLaurenLand, TommyLand, etc. are all wondrous holiday destinations (and in many ways, as 'real' as the mythical 'Paris', 'Venice', 'London', 'Amsterdam' or 'Bali' experienced by the tourist). The added value (and therefore the success) of such 'idea brands' lies in the fact that they explode with so much lifestyle information that is often complex and difficult to verbally articulate, and that the particular vision of how life should/could be which is projected into virtual space is one that pushes enough of the right buttons of belief and desire for a large enough number of consumers with the wherewithal to buy into/'travel to' this dream place.

Interestingly, therefore, successful designer brands and successful regional/national brands are for all intents and purposes the same thing: signifiers of some mythical, utopian place where a particular lifestyle can be pursued without too much reference to the irksome realities of our everyday lives; theme parks where we can get away from it all. (Or, in the atypical case of Benetton in its eighties phase, a place where – rather like heaven – the good life can be achieved by directly addressing the world's ills with good works and right thinking.) Just as the tourist/traveller signals his or her lifestyle profile by sending postcards or emails home from the right geographic brand location, so the fashion consumer, by wearing the right brands, can incorporate within his or her own style statement the lifestyle significations inherent within his or her chosen brand's hypothetical theme park.

There are exceptions (we will consider Diesel in a moment), but for most brands the starting point of their geographical, local branding is – logically enough – their own or their designer's 'actual' region or country of origin. The term 'actual' must appear in quotation marks, of course, because (as per our previous discussion) such places are always semiologically reconfigured to the point that they bear little if any objective relationship to reality – as is vividly demonstrated when contrasting brands from the same country such as Armani and Versace, Vivienne Westwood and Burberry, Tommy Hilfiger and Ralph Lauren. This is because geographic/cultural location is but a backdrop, a screen for the projection of values, beliefs, dreams and desires – the latter always dictating the shape of the former.

upper left: VIVIENNE WESTWOOD, Dressing Up-collection, a/w
lower left: TOMMY HILFIGER, advertising campaign 2004

upper right: 1991 BURBERRY, advertising campaign 2004
lower right: RALPH LAUREN, hand-knitted sweater with short jeans, photo: courtesy Ralph Lauren

For example, a key signification of any design of Vivienne Westwood's is its Englishness. This is not, however, the more traditional and more straightforward vision of the English upper class which Burberry draws upon, but (remarkably like Derek Jarman's juxtaposition of England's future and past in the film *Jubilee*) one which puts English punks and English aristocrats into bed together. (In the same way that Brand London's most popular postcards for tourists depict the Tower of London or Buckingham Palace on the one hand and professional punks on the other – , 'professional' since this style tribe no longer exists in the UK so they are operating as models .) Like Jarman's film, WestwoodLand posits an England which is both very old and very new (postmodern) and where the Queen is both eminently regal and perfectly street credible with a safety pin stuck through her nose.

An alternative juxtaposition of class and street is to be found in Tommy Hilfiger's America, where fair Ivy League preppies can find get-down street cred authenticity and jive-talking black rap artists from the ghetto can discover class. A modern take on a very American dream: everyone gets what they want/need for the pursuit of happiness. Ralph Lauren's America, on the other hand, re-writes history in a different way to give this relatively new country an ancient past with a distinctly European, aristocratic flavour. In this way, magically, the American nouveau riche can achieve old money, Old Europe respectability – and all against the backdrop of a new, vibrant landscape where you can ride on your horse into the sunset. Levi's, however, while once (and logically so) the appearance brand most closely associated with the Wild West, has recently decided to close down this particular American theme park and set up shop in some HipUrbanStreetLand which could be anywhere. This could be a sign of things to come – for as Simon Anholt argues in *Brand America* (Cyan Books, 2004), this national brand may be increasingly loosing its appeal for consumers outside the USA.

While appearance brands such as Westwood, Burberry, Hilfiger, Lauren and (once upon a time) Levi's typically take an existing geographic brand and tweak it to their own ends, Belgian designers like Ann Demeulemeester completely deconstructed (trashed might be another word for it) their existing national brand identity (a sort of country joke; harmless but devoid of cool, sexuality or chic) [6] Like music, art and cinema, design often plays an important part in shaping regional/national brand identities (a role which looks set on growing even more important in the future). However the case of Belgium is truly remarkable in the extent to which a few designers from Antwerp (aided arguably by some techo musicians and DJs) succeeded in so effectively rebranding their country – within only a few years positioning Belgium

(a place previously associated only with mussels, beer, sprouts, bland bureaucrats and Tin Tin) precisely on the cutting edge of the design world as the epitome of cool, sexy, avant-garde sophistication.

A similar rebranding of Italy occurred after the Second World War, and Italian designers have been benefiting ever since. Which makes it very interesting that the Italian brand Diesel has gone out of its way to create the perception that it is anything but Italian. Unlike Benetton's vision of a 'united' global community, Diesel's carefully crafted communication jumps from one stereotypical locality to another until virtually every geographic brand (the American South, Japan, Switzerland, West Indies, India, Africa – everywhere except Italy) has been crammed into Diesel's The World Is Your Oyster theme park, Dieselising the entire planet with a delightfully tacky layering of sticky postmodern irony in the process. An appearance brand which once published an *Essential Words and Phrases for Travellers and Tourists* containing helpful translations for phrases such as 'Please remove the fetid carcass from the bedroom' and 'Her skin has a purple hue', Diesel appears to have deliberately crafted itself as a brand of no fixed abode, one which is perpetually passing through all the world's regional and national brands but steadfastly refusing to settle down. What is particularly interesting about this remarkable brand is that its 'actual' country of abode is Italy – a national brand which fashion companies from practically anywhere else in the world would give the shirt off their backs to be able to legitimately tap into.

It is of course not only in the guise of designer brands that regional/national brands impact upon the world of appearance. Local – usually 'exotic' and traditional – textiles and designs have been spotlighted throughout the long history of fashion as a way of paying a kind of homage to distant lands while, at the same time ultimately underlining the power and glory and reach of Western fashion – celebrating Peruvian peasant embroidery one season, capriciously discarding it as passé the next . The important point for our purposes is this: if fashion experienced a sudden enthusiasm for, say, tartan, Nehru jackets, batik or Hawaiian prints, it did not follow that the Scottish Highlands, India, Java or Hawaii had suddenly become part of the fashion universe. The ultimate empire, fashion consumed stylistic ideas from everywhere but it always did so in a way which scoffed at the very notion that any other part of the world could compete in its league. The very fact that traditional designs, textiles, patterns or colour palettes from across the globe could occasionally be showcased as 'the new look' inarguably demonstrated the extent of its imperialistic power.

upper left: ANN DEMEULEMEESTER, 2003, photo: Dan Lecca
lower left: ISSEY MIYAKE, Pleats Please

upper right: ANN DEMEULEMEESTER, 2002
lower right: WOMAN DRESSED IN KIMONO, Japan

For hundreds of years fashion was unalterably linked to one and only one national brand: France. Each year, dolls called 'Pandoras' (presumably because they were packed in boxes) were each year dressed in the latest designs and dispatched from Paris to would-be chic consumers as far afield as Australia and America. Although in time such dolls were replaced by illustrations and photographs, the same geographic/cultural monoculture prevailed. Only in the second half of the twentieth century did Milan, London and New York successfully (but only to a point) challenge this national brand monopoly.

While the rise of fashion fairs/weeks everywhere from Melbourne to Buenos Aires suggests that expansion beyond Paris, Milan, London and New York is inevitable, the practical difficulties of already jet-lagged journalists and buyers venturing further and further afield remains problematic. Yet a more careful examination of the fashion world reveals that a substantial revolution has already taken place. Namely, Paris in particular has been transformed into a distribution centre for designers from all over the world, with French designers themselves increasingly out in the cold (or, in the case of Gaultier, one suspects, retaining popularity by virtue of the fact that he good-naturedly plays the part of a charming and amusing parody of a Frenchman).

Rather than attempting to pass themselves off as French, a new breed of international designers explicitly underline and celebrate their own particular national origins: Issey Miyake, Rifat Ozbek and Xuly-Bët (to name but a few) unashamedly bringing a bit of Japan, Turkish Cyprus and Mali into the heart of what was once an exclusive club of one. The reasons for this breakthrough of the local into the global are threefold. Firstly, as previously suggested in this essay, there is an increasing appetite for cultural otherness, probably as a reaction against globalisation itself. Secondly, after centuries of Western arrogance, we are at long last being forced to confront as never before the inadequacies in our own culture and are beginning to grasp the undeniable sophistication of other, ancient ways of life. Thirdly, to return to our earlier discussion of recent, dramatic transformations within the fashion system, such a broadening of geographic/cultural scope can be seen as but one consequence of fashion's collapsing centre and the decline of its dictatorial power to enforce a single, unified stylistic direction. While all of the fashion world could agree on Dior's 'New Look' in the late 1940s or Quant's mini in the early 1960s, today there is no such consensus. And within such pluralism there is plenty of room for different national brands as well as different looks.

And surely this is only the beginning. In the long run this hunger for the local (coupled with other stresses and pressures in the fashion system as it struggles to adjust to life in the postmodern age) seems bound to generate a fundamental structural reorganisation which will overshadow even what has gone before. For example, while there are obviously limits to how many countries can become regular stops on the fashion journalists and buyers' twice yearly itinerary, isn't the very idea that all these matt black-clad bodies must physically migrate between shows (the shows themselves prohibitively expensive for new talent) something of an anachronism in the Global Village? Imagine future fashion journalists sitting in their own homes downloading JPEGs and DVDs from – literally – all over the world. And doing so all the time. Of course the fashion establishment will mock such an idea, but in an age when the consumer knows what s/he wants and is increasingly calling the shots, the time may be fast approaching when fashion industry professionals have no choice but to break with the past and plug into the electronic global village in order to provide the buying public with access to designs and designers from every part of the planet.

Meanwhile, how can designers from countries which previously were seen as outside the fashion universe get exposure abroad? With difficulty, would seem to be the obvious answer. A few international competitions for new designers provide opportunities for precious exposure. For example, the Eve organisation's yearly IT'S (1/2/3, with IT'S 4 in 2005) offers the chance for designers from countries as far afield as China, India, Cuba and Russia to come to Trieste in the north of Italy to showcase their work, meet with the international press and, if they win, fund further collections.[7] But more opportunities are desperately needed. Throughout the world a great many countries are pouring money into fashion education, but much of this is wasted and export possibilities are ignored if designers are not given support after graduation to showcase themselves and their work on the international stage.

Given the ever-increasing difficulties facing independent designers everywhere in struggling against the economic clout of international brands, it would seem desirable and cost-effective for designers from outside the main citadels of the fashion industry to be clustered together within the protection of national 'umbrella brands' which, while not restricting them stylistically, could offer logistical support and – essential in today's world – international brand recognition. From a conceptual as well as a financial point of view (and let's not forget, as previously discussed, fashion is now a predominately idea/concept-based industry), the most effective means of accomplishing this would be an interfacing of bodies concerned with the promotion of design with those concerned with the promotion of tourism.

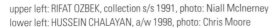

upper left: RIFAT OZBEK, collection s/s 1991, photo: Niall McInerney
lower left: HUSSEIN CHALAYAN, a/w 1998, photo: Chris Moore

upper right: TURKISH WOMEN IN TRADITIONAL GARMENTS
lower right: JOLINE JOLINK, ITS 2 collection, 2003

For most countries design is a key component of national brand identity, which in turn has a crucial part to play in determining how receptive the rest of the world is to its design exports. Typically, this isn't simply a matter of good or bad, yes or no, with the characteristics of each national brand defining a niche of expectations. Brazil, for example, may be a very hot, popular brand throughout the world at the moment, but a Brazilian designer specialising in serious, quality clothes for the work place (in the manner of Armani) would face an uphill struggle, since s/he would be going against the grain of a national brand identity that sees only frolicking on the beach and the fun of carnival. Yet if the rest of the world could see (as I have) that Brazilian designers are producing work which operates effectively outside as well as inside the confines of its current national brand stereotype, this could have the effect of broadening and enriching perceptions of the country as a whole – and an increase in its tourism.[8] In a similar way, Brazil's neighbour Argentina, while also a hot brand at the moment, suffers from the perception that it is stuck in a time warp from the golden age of tango – while, as anyone who has visited Buenos Aires knows, its culture in general and its design in particular is astoundingly contemporary.

Perhaps most important of all, fashion and other designers in 'developing countries' (by which I simply mean countries which have not yet achieved significant international recognition for their design talents) need to have confidence in and reflect their own culture's unique qualities. That is, they need to be local. All too often fashion designers and brands from outside Europe and America have presumed that the secret of success is to be 'international' – suggesting a lack of confidence in the sophistication and appeal of their own local aesthetic sensibilities. In an age when there is a seemingly insatiable hunger for the local in the face of globalisation, such a lack of confidence forfeits a valuable resource (as well as being a recipe for disaster). What might be seen locally as a lack of sophistication is very likely to be perceived from abroad as delightfully fresh, rich and highly desirable – a precious alternative to the lowest common denominator of globalisation. This is not to say that the designers of 'developing countries' should produce work which is a pastiche of their traditional national costume. No, what is needed is a distillation of one's own local design and culture – stripping it down to its fundamental vocabulary – so that its spirit can then be translated into a twenty-first-century, world-wide context without loss of coherence or integrity. Replicate the same process across the planet and the result would be a global village sustained and energised by an astounding diversity, where bland globalisation would have little appeal.

VERONICA WUNDERLIN NEUMAN, ITS 2 collection, 2003

NOTES

[1] How one wishes it were possible to avoid this stupid and geographically meaningless term! But unfortunately we have still to develop adequate replacements for 'the West' and 'Westernisation'. 'Third World', 'developing countries', etc., are even more problematic as they replace geographical inaccuracy with prejudicial notions of superiority and achievement. Far from simply a linguistic problem, this terminological muddle belies a crucial paradigm fault. Are we (whoever 'we' are!) justified in presuming *any* kind of distinction between 'us' and 'them' in the twenty-first century?

[2] As an American who has long resided in Britain, I never cease to be amazed at the frequency with which even 'serious' broadsheet newspapers in the UK run articles that delight in reporting some survey which suggests that people in France use less soap than people in the UK. The cultural foundations of all notions of cleanliness are explored in the anthropologist Mary Douglas's book *Purity and Danger: An Analysis of Pollution and Taboo* (Penguin Books, 1970).

[3] Readers of my other works will know that I am of the view that these changes have been so extreme and systemic that it would be advantageous to switch from 'fashion' to 'style' as a term for describing the appearance industries. To do so here, however, may cause confusion.

[4] In truth, throughout all of human history appearance has served as a crucial communication system; it has always been a 'statement'. What has changed is that (1) such 'fashion statements' are now much more personal constructions created by individual consumers and (2) while once such visual messages were relatively straightforward ('I'm an aristocrat', 'I'm the chief of this tribe', 'I'm respectable') they are now often extraordinarily complex symbols of personal attitude, belief, philosophy, ethics and dreams. It should also be pointed out that an emphasis on statement does not obliterate concern for the aesthetic: that which says the right things will also 'look nice'.

[5] The phrase 'presentation of self' comes from the sociologist Irving Goffman. For our purposes it should be appreciated that one's presentation of self is made up of a wide range of separate components: clothing, accessories, hair and cosmetics styles, glasses/sunglasses, tattoos or piercings, jewellery, one's choice of bottled beverage, a dog, one's car, etc. As appearance becomes more explicitly preoccupied with 'statement' — what it has to say, message as opposed to medium — the logic of fencing off clothing as a separate industry seems increasingly suspect.

[6] As with most of the national stereotypes presented here, this view of Belgium is one which was prevalent in Britain and America. I cannot say whether it is consistent with those stereotypes that prevailed in other countries. It goes without saying that, as with so many of the geographic mythologies included here, it was far from an objective portrayal of Belgium — a country which, in truth, has had a long established tradition of design creativity.

[7] www.itsweb.org for further details. IT'S is sponsored by Diesel, amongst others.

[8] This view of Brazilian design is shared by *Wallpaper Navigator* magazine's Spring/Summer 04 edition. For my experiences visiting Argentina and Brazil (which in both instances substantially contributed to the development of this essay) I am indebted to Vicky Salías of Centro Metropolitano de Diseño in BA and Cristiane Mesquita of SENAC in SP.

BIBLIOGRAPHY

Anolt, Simon – BRAND AMERICA – Cyan Books, 2004.

Baudot, Francois – A CENTURY OF FASHION – Thames & Hudson, 1999.

Goffman, Erving – THE PRESENTATION OF SELF IN EVERYDAY LIFE – Doubleday, 1956.

McLuhan, Marshall – THE GUTENBERG GALAXY: THE MAKING OF TYPOGRAPHIC MAN – University of Toronto Press, 1962.

Polhemus, Ted – DIESEL: WORLD WIDE WEAR – Watson-Guptill Publications, 1998.

Polhemus, Ted – STYLE SURFING: WHAT TO WEAR IN THE 3RD MILLENNIUM – Thames & Hudson, 1996.

Sillitoe, Alan – LEADING THE BLIND: A CENTURY OF GUIDE BOOK TRAVEL 1815-1914 – Macmillan, 1995.

Urry, John – CONSUMING PLACES – Routledge, 1995.

Urry, John – THE TOURIST GAZE: LEISURE AND TRAVEL IN CONTEMPORARY SOCIETIES – Sage Publications, 1990.

GLOBAL FASHION BASED ON LOCAL TRADITION

For two hundred years fashion was a Western and almost exclusively Parisian affair. In the 1980s, however, Paris grew into a multicultural platform where designers from many different countries and regions of the world were welcome to show their work. It is striking that since that time many designers have been harking back to their own culture's traditions and clothing customs and then translating them into advanced and fashionable designs. A representative selection of these is being shown in the exhibition.

XULY BËT

Xuly Bët, pronounced 'hoolic but', is Malinese for 'keep your eyes open'. The man behind the label is Laminee Kouyate (born in Bamako, Mali, 1962). After completing his studies at the art academy in Dakar he went to France to study architecture, but eventually decided to design clothes instead of buildings.

In 1989 he founded Xuly Bët and opened a shop, the Funkin Fashion Factory, in the former X-ray department of an old Paris hospital. His designs were made from second-hand clothes which he took apart and put together again in his own totally different way. Nowadays there are other idealistic businesses that work in this manner, but in 1989 it was revolutionary. Typical of his clothes are the visible seams, the fabrics turned inside out, the use of red threads and the label placed on the outside. After he had

first successfully conquered the hip Parisian youth market, the rest of the world followed suit and he currently has shops all over the world. In the meantime the demand for his clothing has become so great that it is no longer feasible to make it all from second-hand fabrics and materials. But a small percentage of his collection still makes use of second-hand clothing.

Xuly Bët is regarded as typically African because of his use of the principle of recycling. He himself said in an interview in NRC Handelsblad in 1996, 'What is African about Xuly Bët? Myself. Everything. Nothing. Africa is seen here as a dark spot on the map where only bad things come from. But Africa is moving. Young Africans are open to the world and they have big aspirations.' What is African in his work, Kouyate says, lies not so much in the recycling principle as in the mes-

sage he is spreading, including the use of African fabrics: Africa is up and coming. MF

DRESS a/w 2004/2005
collection Centraal Museum
One of the features of Xuly Bët is the text 'Xuly Bët's Funking Fashion' that he occasionally prints on his fabrics in large letters. This dress made of voile-like, transparent plastic is printed with the familiar Xuly Bët logo in gold.

VIVIENNE WESTWOOD

Vivienne Westwood (England, 1941) appeared on the international fashion stage in 1971 when she and Malcolm McLaren opened a shop on Kings Road. Her designs set the trend for the punk movement in the seventies, partly through the success of the punk band The Sex Pistols, discovered by McLaren.

During her collaboration with McLaren she looked back into English history and was inspired by the Teddy Boys from the fifties. In the early eighties she left the punk movement and switched to English costume history as the guideline for her designs, using a great deal of tweed, Scottish checks and traditional English cutting techniques in her creations. Besides her references to British culture, the themes of power and eroticism play a major role in her designs. The focus is on the female form, emphasised and even exaggerated. For, as Vivienne Westwood herself says, 'A woman is by definition sexy when she looks important.'

During her career, Vivienne Westwood has gone from anarchist to British role model. From 1989 until 1991 she was professor of fashion in Vienna and she currently teaches in Berlin. She received the British Designer of the Year award in 1990 and 1991 and received an OBE in 1992. The Victoria and Albert Museum in London organised a retrospective exhibition of her work in 2004. MF

VIVIENNE WEST WOOD, Baseballshirt s/s 2002

www.viviennewestwood.co.uk

COMME DES GARÇONS

Rei Kawakubo (Tokyo, 1942) studied at the art academy in Tokyo and worked as a stylist for a number of years after graduating. In 1969 she founded Comme des Garçons, which grew into a flourishing business in Japan. The first shop opened in 1975 and in 1978 Kawakubo started a new men's line.

Her designs concentrate on the feminine image and traditional notions of beauty. She doesn't think it's sexy to reveal the body and so you won't find sensual accents on the buttocks, breasts or legs in her designs.

When Rei Kawakubo showed for the first time in Paris in 1981, her designs were seen by the press as a direct challenge to Western aesthetics. But her designs are more than just a critique of Western taste; conceptually they are very strong and explore the existing forms of a garment by experi-menting with it. She makes clothes with one sleeve missing, for example, or places the pockets upside down. Initially her designs were only executed in various shades of black and grey, the very colours that were unpopular at the time. More colour is used in her later collections, but she continues to be provocative. In 1997, for example, she produced a collection in which she questions 'ideal' body proportions. Padding the clothes made it look as if the models had humps, or crooked or gigantic hips. Since she has a number of commercial sidelines in Japan, Kawakubo can afford to continue working experimentally. In 1983 she won the Mainichi Fashion Grand Prize and in 1987 the Fashion Institute of Technology declared her one of the most prominent female designers of the twentieth century. MF

SWEATER, SKIRT AND LEGGING
a/w 1999/2000
collection Centraal Museum
In this collection Rei Kawakubo of Comme des Garçons experiments with the limits of an article of clothing. An existing skirt and sweater are taken apart and arbitrarily put together again.

OUTDOOR DRESS, S/S 1997
collection Boijmans van Beuningen
In 1997 Rei Kawakubo launched a collection in which she experimented with feminine forms. Why should curves always be on the buttocks and breasts and not on other parts of the body? The collection flies in the face of the dominant aesthetic, and the press associated the strange look more with Quasimodo than with beauty.

BERNHARD WILHELM

Bernhard Wilhelm (Ulm, 1972) studied fashion design at the University of Trier in 1993 and 1994 before deciding to continue his education in Antwerp at the Royal Academy of Fine Art. There, in a design competition organised by the magazine Knack in 1996, he won the prize for the most innovative collection. He then worked as an intern for Vivienne Westwood, Alexander McQueen and Dirk Bikkembergs. That he is a remarkable talent was evident in 1998 when he presented his final exam collection, 'Le petit Chapeau Rouge', which drew a great deal of media attention. Typical of Wilhelm's designs are the handiwork, the embroidery and the knitting he applies to mostly casual clothes like jogging sets or butterfly sweaters. Decorative socks, shawls and hats have become an original Bernhard Wilhelm trademark, since he likes to play with the homemade fashion culture of the sev-

enties. His Bavarian background can be seen in his predilection for knitting, embroidery and in socks with naive figurative prints.

Right after his final exams Wilhelm was asked by the Japanese firm Minimam to work on the Young Generation Designers Project, for which he designed both a men's collection and a women's collection. In 1999 Bernhard Wilhelm started his own women's collection and immediately presented it in Paris, where it was enthusiastically received. In the meantime he has designed a men's line and his collection is on sale in several countries. In 2002 he was asked to breathe new life into the Italian fashion house of Roberto Capucci. In the same year the German Ursula Blickle Stiftung organised an exhibition and book about his work under the title 'Moderne Mode', pre-

senting a survey of his work since 1999. MF

JACKET WITH LONG SOCKS AND LION HAT, a/w 2005/2006
collection Centraal Museum
Wilhelm's inspiration for this collection came from Paris's African street culture and the way the people there use colour. This time he emphasises the family and domestic qualities of his collection by incorporating photos and drawings by his assistants as a running theme .

SHIRT AND SKIRT, s/s 2005
collection Centraal Museum
This skirt and top were completely embroidered with exquisite little figures and decorated with beads.

BERNARD WILLHELM, s/s 2005

BERNARD WILLHELM, Shirt and skirt, s/s 2005

HUSSEIN CHALAYAN

Hussein Chalayan (born in Nicosia, 1970) studied at the Türk Maarif College in Nicosia. After graduating he left for London where he continued his education at the Central Saint Martins College of Art and Design. There he presented his final exam collection in 1993, 'The Tangent Flows', which consisted of clothes he had buried for three months in his back garden so the material was badly damaged. He started his own label in 1994 and won a design competition organised by Absolut Vodka in 1995. With the prize money he was able to design a collection for the London Fashion Week.

In 1999 and 2000 he received the British Designer of the Year award. He has now been in the business for ten years, a jubilee that is being celebrated in the spring of 2005 with a one-man show in the Groningen Museum and the publication of a monograph.

Twice a year Chalayan presents a wearable men's and women's collection in Paris, but he is best known for his experimental installations at these shows. His work is characterised by the fact that, unlike most other fashion designers, he is inspired not so much by fashion history but by philosophy, architecture, politics and anthropology. This, in combination with his fascination for new technology, results in an innovative use of materials and experimental forms. Examples of these are a letter that can be folded out into a paper dress, a coffee table that changes into a skirt, and clothes made of fibreglass.

Hussein Chalayan's conceptual designs are a response to political, social and cultural affairs and often refer to his own Turkish-Cypriot background. His heritage can be seen more in his ideas than in his actual designs.

In recent years he has been developing more and more projects that are independent of fashion, such as the video installation Place to Passage (2004). At the moment he is showing his ideas and installations mostly in the art circuit, restricting himself on the catwalk to a wearable clothing line. MF

TWO OUTFITS FROM AMBIMORPHOUS,
a/w 2002/2003
on loan
Hussein Chalayan's Ambimorphous is based on traditional Turkish/Ottoman costume. The collection started with a model in traditional costume, and with each subsequent model a piece of the costume was replaced by a black area, eventually resulting in simple, wearable clothes whose lines followed those of the original Turkish costume.

HUSSEIN CHALAYAN, Ambimorphous, a/w 2002/2003

ALEXANDRE HERCHCOVITCH

'It's a cliché to say that clothes are a means of expression, a code for communicating something specific. Anyone wearing one of my designs is transmitting information about the way he or she sees the world. I'm not so interested in the model, the length or the colour of clothing. I am much more concerned with establishing a dialogue between my universe and that of my clients.'

Alexandre Herchcovitch (São Paolo, 1971) feels like a modern world citizen in South America. His grandparents were Polish, he went to a Orthodox Jewish school in São Paolo and later studied at a Catholic fashion academy. With such a mixture of cultures and backgrounds, typical of many South Americans, it's not surprising that he mixes all sorts of influences and styles in his designs. 'My mother had a lingerie factory and that's where my interest in fashion was awakened. When I started following international fashion in the eighties I was interested in the conceptual creations of Comme des Garçons, but also in the super-feminine silhouettes of Thierry Mugler. My own style is typified by a search for combinations.'

If you look at Herchcovitch's work of the last ten years you'll see that his collections do indeed consist of graphic and formal experiments, combined with feminine and smoothly draping clothes. A second leitmotif in his work is the use of rubber from the Amazonian rubber tree. He uses the liquid rubber to make splendid hand-painted patterns that fall around the body, almost like lacework.

Herchcovitch has a number of shops of his own in Brazil and now sells his creations all over the world. In 2000 he launched three collections in London and showed for the first time in Paris. At the moment he is one of Brazil's most important designers; every six months he presents a women's, men's and jeans line at the São Paolo Fashion Week. His show in Paris has now been swapped for a show in New York since there the market is more commercially attractive. AS

DRESS, a/w 2004/2005
on loan
Dress made of black rubber. In this collection Alexandre Herchcovitch plays lightly with surrealism by giving the models hats of black, abstracted fruit.

DRESS, a/w 2005/2006
on loan
The dress is made of liquid rubber formed with a brush. Little red hearts and yellow birds form a sort of openwork motif in the transparent skirt.

ALEXANDRE HERCHCOVITCH, Dress, a/w 2005/2006

SOPHIA KOKOSALAKI

Sophia Kokosalaki (Athens, 1972) studied Greek literature at the University of Athens and earned her diploma in 1998 at the Central Saint Martins College of Art and Design in London. Kokosalaki's chief interest is in the past, particularly the Greek clothing tradition of drapery and sophisticated Greek embroidery. She manages to translate these techniques into elegant, feminine dresses with loosely falling drapes and decorated with delicate embroidery. She is even able to pleat, braid and knot a material such as leather as though it were embroidery. That delicate feel for handiwork, which also occurs in her sophisticated draperies, gives her designs a timeless elegance. Or, as she describes it herself, 'My designs are complex and labour-intensive, but at the same time they are also graceful and contemporary.'

Since 2000 Kokosalaki has been showing her collections in London and established a certain name for herself there. In 2001 she won the Elle Style Award for 'Best New Designer', and in 2002 the Art Foundation Award for Fashion. She became known to the public at large in 2003 when she was allowed to make a small collection for Top Shop. But more than anything else it was the Ocean Dress she designed for Björk when she was chief designer for the Olympic Games in Greece in 2004 that really made her famous. When she decided to do a show in Paris in October 2004, the international press threw themselves on her as the latest hype.

In this collection she translates details from the sea into an undulating blue dress with appliquéd anemones on the shoulders and a silk jersey in watery blue and pale pink colours. AS

SOPHIA KOKOSALAKI, a/w 2005/2006

SOPHIA KOKOSALAKI, a/w 2005/2006

SOPHIA KOKOSALAKI, a/w 2005/2006

YOHJI YAMAMOTO

Yohji Yamamoto (Ioyko, 1943) graduated in 1969 from the Banka Fashion Academy in Tokyo. In 1972 he founded Yohji Yamamoto Ltd. and gave his first show in Tokyo in 1977. Yamamoto feels that fashion should be human. Many of his designs are asymmetrical, since he sees symmetry as the symbol of perfection and therefore not human. Searching for its essence also makes clothing more human , the showy elements of fashion being merely a masquerade. Designing is 'thinking about people', says Yamamoto. For example, 'How do people decide whether, and to what extent, they want to stand out or to be swallowed up in the group?' He is particularly interested in schoolgirls' uniforms, for although they all look the same, the details ensure that some girls stand out in the group – through a buttoned-up blouse, or through a few buttons left open, or because of an accessory.
www.yohjiyamamoto.co.jp

This philosophy leads to sober designs, often totally black. Yet Yamamoto's creations are never boring. By draping fabric around a model like a sculptor he creates new and interesting forms. Initially his designs comprised several layers of loose-fitting black clothing, but his style later became less loose-fitting, sometimes with a touch of colour. MF

DRESS/JACKET a/w 2005/2006
collection Centraal Museum
The woollen jacket is a cross between an evening gown and a jacket. By applying simple seams to the somewhat stiff wool an almost frivolous feminine line is created, especially because of the wide '1830' sleeves and the use of chandelier drops and studs as decoration.

DRESS a/w s/s 2000
collection Centraal Museum
This design is Yohji Yamamoto's answer to the revival of haute couture. Its basis is a 'Western' waisted dress made of testing cotton in which the basted seams serve as decoration. On top of this Yamamoto has placed a draped piece of cloth attached to the back with ribbons in the Japanese manner.

ISSEY MIYAKE

Issey Miyake (Hiroshima, 1938) graduated in 1964 from the Tama Art
University in Tokyo as a graphic designer. After this he left for Paris where he
applied himself to couture and worked
with Guy Laroche and Hubert Givenchy.
In 1971 he presented his first collection in both Tokyo and New York. In
1973 he tried his luck in Paris and since
then he has been showing his designs
twice a year. Issey Miyake thinks that
clothes should flow over the body
instead of being constructed on it. In
typically Japanese fashion he bases
himself on the texture of the fabric and
the way it falls, and only then thinks of
the body.

In 1993 Miyake introduced his 'Pleats
Please' concept to the market, a line of
clothing made from a high tech, pleated polyester, with a pleating technique
that goes back to an ancient Japanese
principle. These garments are ideal for
www. isseymiyake.com

travel, since they give the body great
deal of freedom of movement, don't
crease and can be machine washed
and dried in an hour. Because of their
ultimate comfort, Miyake regards the
'Pleats Please' line as the jeans of the
future.

In 1999 Miyake and Dai Fujiwara presented a second revolutionary concept:
A-POC (A Piece of Cloth), a design principle whereby the form of a garment is
already woven into a piece of cloth by
means of moulding technology. A dress
can be cut from it with long or short
sleeves, a knee-length skirt or a mini-
skirt. The combination of the latest
technologies with ancient traditions
and customs is what makes Miyake so
special. MF

DRESS AND SHAWL, s/s 2001
This pleated chemise and shawl are both made
of double-stitched fabric. The fabric of both the
dress and the shawl is filled with tiny figures
made of black tulle that move about freely in the
fabric – like down in a duvet . They give the dress
and the shawl a nice volume in the bottom hem.

A-POC 'KANAZAWA' s/s 2005
This piece of cloth was designed for the opening
of the Century Museum of Contemporary Art in
Kanazawa in 2004. It is a stylised version of the
museum's floor plan. Seven pieces can be cut out
of it – a skirt, a cape, gloves, socks and a cushion
– which exactly follow the lines of the museum's
walls. The series was developed to celebrate the
fifth anniversary of A-POC.

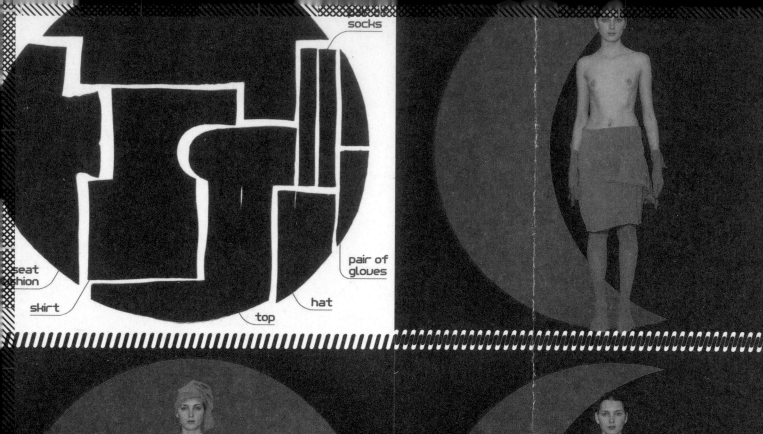

socks

pair of
gloves

seat
cushion

skirt   top   hat

ISSEY MIYAKE, A-POC 'Kanazawa' s/s 2005

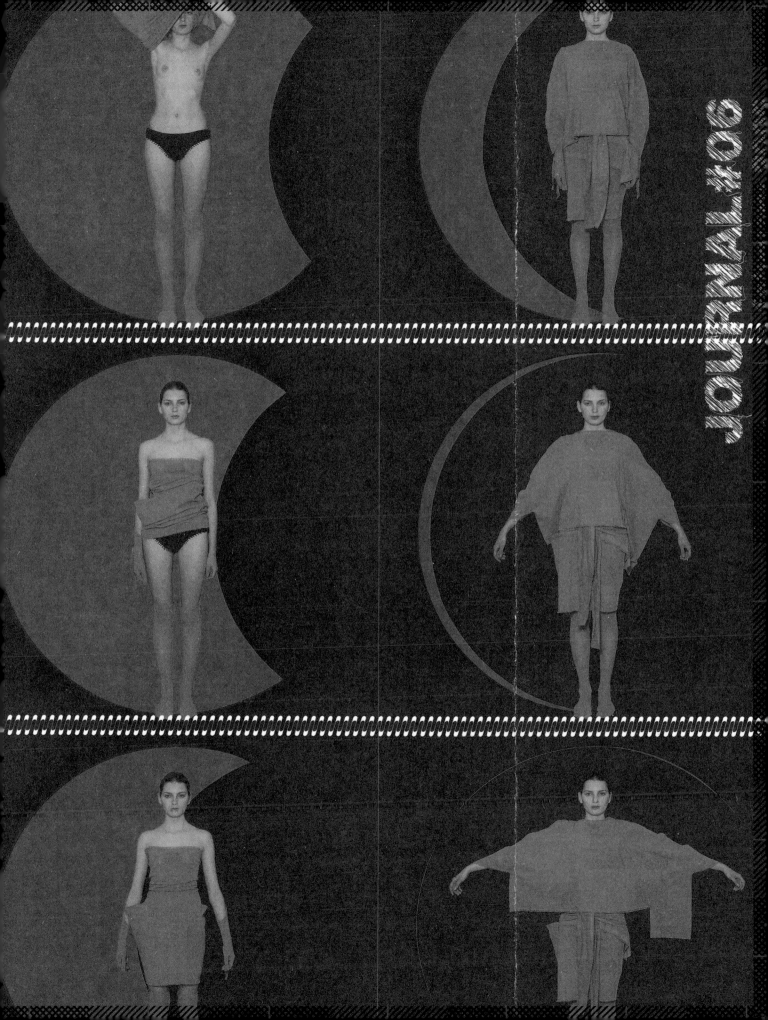

JUNYA WATANABE

Junya Watanabe (1961) graduated from the Bunka Fashion Institute in Tokyo in 1984 and went to work for Comme des Garçons under the guidance of Rei Kawakubo, who quickly realised that Junya was very talented and enabled him to start his own label within her fashion house in 1992. For Junya Watanabe this meant that Comme des Garçons took care of his financing, distribution, sales and publicity, while he was given a completely free hand in designing.

What characterises Watanabe's collections is that his designs feature more than just one style. Each collection is totally different from the next, which makes it surprising. He sets himself challenges and arrives at groundbreaking forms by endlessly experimenting with techniques. As a result his garments are always very innovative and non-compromising: a jacket

that can be folded back into a handbag and lengths of felt that end up in three-dimensional forms not by cutting but by spiralling. His designs do not focus on a theme or a special type of woman. 'Sometimes I come across things when designing that don't let go of me and which I then experiment and develop into a new collection,' says Watanabe. In 2001 he started his own men's line, which has been very successful. MF

LAVENDER-COLOURED DRESS, a/w 2000/2001
collection Centraal Museum
For this collection Junya Watanabe made a series of dresses from ultramodern polyester, with layers of fabric stitched together. This lilac dress is an oval form onto which 50 layers have been loosely stitched. By draping the length of cloth around the waist and neck and closing the only snap, it turns into a splendid dress.

TOP, s/s 2005
Top made of black, pleated washed cotton. Collar and cuffs are thickened with several layers of unfinished fabric.

JUNYA WATANABE, Lavender-coloured dress; a/w 2000/2001

ROY VILLEVOYE

RETURNING
1992 - 1995, 1997

The first time I went to Asmat in Papua, which was in 1992, I decided to take a few T-shirts with me as presents. They were just ordinary white T-shirts but in my studio I had punched 24 holes into the front and back of each shirt. I then surrounded each hole with a skin-coloured circle of make-up. It was the result of a long process on which I had been working as an artist; an attempt to make a tangible painting and to give a new meaning to it in the commonplace.

Whoever accepted such a T-shirt as a present would, by putting it on, complete the work of art by placing the world-wide range of skin colours against his own skin colour. Excitedly, I took a few photos when the first person donned his present.

After returning home, I started to live with those photos and I kept asking myself who that man was.

Three years later I returned to his little settlement in the rain forest, in the hope of meeting him once more. On arrival, I heard that the man, Foyalé Givanep, had died some time previously. When, subsequently, they showed me the remains of the T-shirt I had given him I felt bewildered. So I exchanged it for the shirt I was wearing and took it home with me. Later, I had my photo taken wearing that same T-shirt, as a tribute to that man and also to allay the confusion I felt.
It took two years before I then could put together the collection of photos.

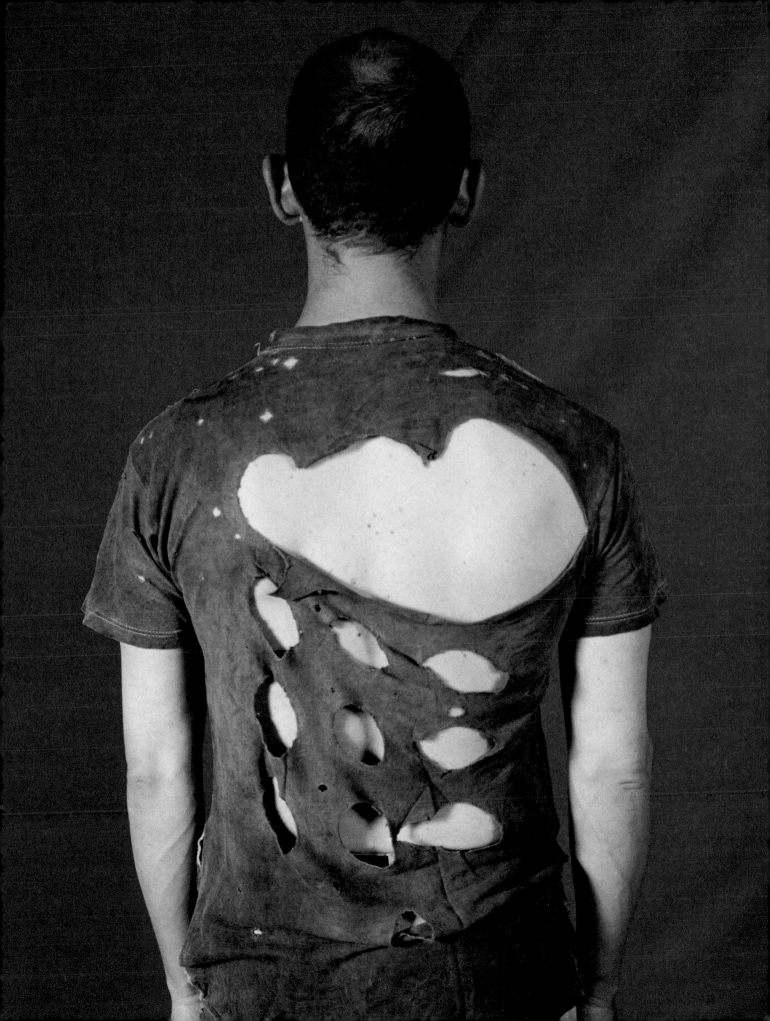

Gosewijn van Beek

CULTURE IN SHREDS

(…)

Then in the late afternoon we sailed up the Oetoemboewe-river and at 1 pm. moored near a creek where some houses had been in December 1904. Now no trace of these were left. When sailing up the river several prows with natives rowed towards us. The moment we showed pieces of red calico, they approached the ship and soon a lively barter was going on. We gave red calico in exchange for several ethnographic objects.

(…)

It is hard to imagine how keen the people are about red calico. Strips of cloth about 3 to 4 cm. wide and 30 to 40 cm long, as long as they were red, were sufficient to acquire arrows and spears, all they had in fact. Several spears were quite artfully decorated. They did not know knives. Offered a choice between a knife and a piece of red cotton, they preferred the latter. *Iron was completely unknown to them*. The same with mirrors. They were indifferent to beads (blue and white). But everything red took their fancy. An empty matchbox with a red and yellow label bought us a bunch of arrows.

Oetoemboewe-river (present Asewetsj, Asmat) 3-4 V 1906,

J.H. HONDIUS VAN HERWERDEN,
Commander of the Gov.'s-S.S. "Valk"
Een verkenningsreis der zuidwestkust van Nieuw-Guinea, van Straat Prinses Marianne tot de Providentiaal-bank; dd. 23 april-8 mei 1906.
(TKNAG 23 (1906) 5, 919-923)

Oetoemboewe .4.5.'06.

Long ago is far away. Once upon a time the encounter with other peoples and cultures was regarded as an exciting enterprise of European discovery. Travellers were unashamed collectors and taxonomists of exotic habits, weird practices and quaint views. Old travelogues of discovery still testify to this zoological approach to the exotic other. In their observations the authors habitually commented on the primitiveness and the naiveté of the natives. Ironically, in our day and age this naiveté has turned against these travellers themselves. Their travelogues now strike us as naive expressions of bias and prejudice.

In the early nineteenth century, the naturalist Lesson joined one such famous voyage of discovery, commissioned by the French government. He boarded the corvette La Coquille under Captain d'Urville and travelled around the world, visiting the still largely unknown islands of New Guinea and the Pacific. In 1839 he published the forth and final volume of his extensive travelogue. It is an entertaining account, yet reading it one is embarrassed as well as humbled. Like those of most of his contemporaries, his observations of other peoples and places are often prejudiced and ethnocentric. There is no doubt, however, that he also was an astute and intelligent observer who took a genuine interest in the daily lives of the people he met. The humility comes when we ourselves, while reading, are confronted with our own private prejudices. I can hardly suppress a smile on seeing my own bias confirmed when this savant explorer writes: '*Le premier art qu'un doive examiner chez tous les peuples, quelle que soit leur civilisation, est celui de la cuisine*'.[1] A Frenchman, certainly! Not surprisingly perhaps he continues to criticise *les naturels* (as he calls the Papuans) for not having made great progress in the culinary department. Again and again he returns to this 'French' theme, quoting with passion a compatriot who observed that '*Le sauvage dévore, l'homme demi-civilisé mange, mais l'homme très civilisé seul sait manger*'.[2]

It may be wise not to criticise Lesson too harshly. Nowadays we think ourselves quite sophisticated in our catholic appreciation of all things ethnic: world cuisine, world music and world aesthetics. The discovery of other people and cultures has become a matter of buying a ticket or turning on Discovery Channel. But we might still shrink from an offering of some fresh larvae or tarantulas with baked sago with a few slimy leaves on the side. Such a world dish offered in the midst of New Guinea might still be a step too far in our determination to embrace otherness. We would probably also shrink from adopting styles of dress that are fashionable with the authentic other. This goes for penis gourds and leaf-skirts, but maybe even more for the dirty, dishevelled and torn shirts that once, when freshly made, looked very different and stylish: T-shirts.

To ironise Lesson would be patronising, as patronising as he was about the Papuans he met about two centuries ago. Excusing him as a child of his times would suggest that we are grown-up moderns who know the harm of prejudice and have freed ourselves from them. In fact, his diary is in many ways a joy of common sense – coloured of course, but genuine in his effort to be a faithful observer and scientist. Ironically, this common sense might still be seen by others as prejudice when he comments on an institution much closer to home: museums. Like his fellow travellers, Lesson was an avid collector. One day, having hunted successfully for zoological and ethnographical specimens, he wryly notes that these probably will end up in '… *le vaste gouffre, appelé en France Muséum, gouffre qui, semblable au tonneau des Danaïdes, recoit sans cesse mais retient peu*'.[3] It is a sentiment that is echoed time and again by critics of the Western museum project. And who would not sympathise, knowing that the total collections of all the world's museums presently amount to billions rather than millions, while 95 percent of this frightening heap will never surface again to be shown in public? At the very least, if we talk about the cultural heritage we now jealously protect (and hide) in ethnological museums, we should remind ourselves that most of it was brought together by politically incorrect researchers like Lesson.

The prejudice of culture and the culture of collecting. Guided by these two anthropological themes distilled from Lesson's travelogue, we must try to make sense of a collection of T-shirts that Lesson would have thought exceedingly weird and exotic, not – perhaps – as ethnographic artefacts, but as collectibles and above all as objects of art. That dirty and torn Western dresses worn by Papuans would one day be exhibited in an ethnographic museum would probably have struck him as quite esoteric, possibly even as brazen. That they would be part of an art project would certainly have been beyond his comprehension. The question is: if we are honest with ourselves, is our reaction any different?

FROM RICHES TO RAGS
The images Roy Villevoye took of Papuan men and women in torn T-shirts, and his mannequins silently parading in the same shirts, pose some thorny problems of prejudice and meaning.

We are looking at Asmat men and women. The Asmat people live on the coastal plains of Southern Papua (Irian Jaya). As a group they are famous the world over for their unique wood-sculpting tradition. No self-respecting ethnographic museum can do without some examples of their sculpture, preferably one of the spectacular *bisj*-poles.[4] With respect to this aesthetic fame, the location of Roy Villevoye's parade of poorly

dressed mannequins – the Leiden Ethnographical Museum – is rather ironic, for it is this very museum that prides itself in having one of the finest collections of Asmat art in the world, much of it brought together by the late Adrian Gerbrands. A former curator of the Leiden museum, Gerbrands was the first to make an extensive study of this remarkable aesthetic tradition, about which he published a landmark study and produced an intriguing documentary film.[5]

The European image of the Asmat is one of a people with a distinct identity, with a strong sense of style in aesthetics and beliefs. That is the way we prefer to see them: as a group of people that still have a sense of community, a closely-knit people supported by shared values and customs that are the result of age-old adaptations to their environment. Such an authentic lifestyle would, of course, defy the superficial attractions of Western fashions, mass-consumption and wilful individualism. Unfortunately, Roy Villevoye's collection and images do not seem to support such romantic expectations. They are disturbing because they uncover a deep ambivalence in our judgement of others and ourselves. Traditionally the Asmat dressed rather scantily. Asmat men in fact walked around virtually naked. Yet, as we know from Gerbrands's pictures from the 1960s, their appearance was stylish, powerful and recognisably their own. But here we are confronted with people dressed in Western rags, an image of Third World poverty and dejection we are all too familiar with. We seem to be looking at a Salvation Army appeal, a poverty parade.

It may have something to do with fact that nowadays the Asmat prefer shirts rather than their customary scanty dress, that our initial reaction is one of disappointment mixed with shame. We are disappointed because nobody apparently can withstand the superficial glamour of Western goods, even when these may be unnecessary, ugly or worn-out. We are ashamed because it is our own doing that made these people hanker after goods they do not need, cannot pay for or do not use properly. What we think we are seeing is globalisation in action, the homogenisation of the world, which will be the undoing of local cultures that once took pride in their rooted traditions.[6]

But we shouldn't be carried away by mere appearances. Our initial judgement may hide a prejudice comparable to Lesson's encounter with the unfamiliar and ill-understood. As a matter of fact, it may well be that we hold a number of misconceptions about our own behaviour with respect to mass consumer goods that cloud a proper interpretation of the Asmat fashion of dressing in supposedly inauthentic second-hand rags. Perhaps we need to have a closer look at the Western history of the T- shirt to see the actual complexities of meaning that

have transformed this simple piece of cotton into the ubiquitous casual dress of modern society.

AMERICAN THINGS

T-shirts are classic American artefacts. As far back as the early twentieth century they were being popularised across America as cheap mass-produced underwear through mail order catalogues like Sears & Roebuck and Montgomery Ward.[7] As such they became part of the standard dress of the US army and navy. Through numerous World War II movies the T-shirt acquired a distinct image. It became associated with being at ease, being unconcerned about class conventions, being workmanlike and democratic. Most of all it stood for youth, toughness and masculinity. These war movies also initiated a shift in the potential of the T-shirt as clothing. Originally meant as an undergarment, apparently it could also be used as a casual outer garment.

In 1950s this image of the T-shirt was transported to Europe by movie icons such as Marlon Brando, Montgomery Clift and James Dean. In crossing the ocean, however, the meaning of the T-shirt was transformed, or to be more precise, another strong 'European' message was added to the T-shirt: that of American-ness. It shared this post-war American association with other iconic consumer items like Coca-Cola, streamlined cars and bubble gum. As such it became part of a fierce controversy over the feared demise of European culture in the onslaught of American superficiality and materialism. Probably because of this, the T-shirt became an ideal trademark for angry young authors like the Dutch writers Jan Cremer and Jan Wolkers. European rebels with or without a cause adopted it along with blue jeans, signifying youth culture as a protest against the established morality of their parents' bourgeois society. Paradoxically, left wing anti-American protesters who demonstrated in the capitals of Europe against the Vietnam War could therefore be dressed in the very T-shirts and blue jeans that were iconic of the American way of life![8]

Then in the eighties the use and meaning of the T-shirt went through another transformation. Its potential as a messenger – carrying texts and logos of all kinds – enabled it to be used as a means of corporate and individual expression which was exploited by small printing industries. As before, the T-shirt could be used in an iconoclastic way, but its American associations had faded, as had its association with youthful protest. We could say that the T-shirt was being localised, becoming part of numerous local subcultures of expression that could not easily be transferred to other places. The famous T-shirt print shop in the Damstraat in Amsterdam featured artist-designed, subversive, often scabrous prints that amazed tourists as 'typically Amsterdam' and that probably wouldn't be tolerated in public anywhere else.

The lesson of this brief history is that mass consumer goods – even though they might be introduced elsewhere and initially be alien to a particular cultural world – often will be transformed in unexpected ways to take on new local cultural meanings. The basic uniformity of the T-shirt as dress all over the world really is a mirage. In the modern world the T-shirt has become ubiquitous casual wear, but wearing it does not necessarily associate us with America, youth culture, rebellion or hard work. In anthropological parlance, it has been appropriated as a versatile vehicle for local identity construction. Or in other words: we have 'captured' the T-shirt from its former 'alien' American symbolism and transformed it into a pluriform garment that we experience as truly our own.

CLOTH AND CLOTHING

This is something we should ponder before we denounce the adoption of Western dress by others. With this cautionary tale in mind, we are ready to look again at New Guinea. Actually the Asmat are not the only group in Melanesia who have taken a fancy to this garment for the masses. The T-shirt is highly popular all over the island, and in fact has been so for many decades. Back in the late seventies, when I conducted research on the independent eastern part of the island, it already was the common modern dress for men in town and village. Everybody who could afford it owned one, preferably one with a fanciful decoration or text. Institutions like the National Museum and Art Gallery in the capital Port Moresby had T-shirts made with their logos to be distributed to all staff as Christmas presents. They were gone within minutes of the director announcing their arrival. Small print shops produced a variety of creative local designs. Thus one could encounter sturdy Papuans on the streets of the town announcing in bold letters 'Jesus lives', children advertising South Pacific as 'the best beer of Papua New Guinea', as well as front /back puns like 'I am looking at your back / I am only looking'.[9] No doubt there was more to this T-shirt fashion than a mere craze for or imitation of Western things, even though the image of being 'modern' and in touch with the wider (Western) world certainly did play a part in the popularity of the dress.

Taking one step back in time, cloth has always been a highly popular object of exchange between Papuan groups and the outside world, along with shells and steel adzes. Even before the arrival of the first European discoverers, traders from the Moluccas introduced woven cloth or *kain timur* from the Indonesian archipelago to the western most parts of New Guinea.[10] The advent of European domination in this area and elsewhere in Melanesia saw traders and missionaries

exchange black, blue and red cotton cloth or calico for local produce, among other things.[11] In contrast to the Indonesian *kain timur*, however, which became a valuable commodity in traditional bride-price exchanges, European calico was used for a variety of decorative or adornment purposes. Thus for a long time now the coastal areas of New Guinea have been exposed to the introduction of similar items, and many of them, such as steel adzes, did find their way to inland areas long before the actual 'first contact' was made with these 'undiscovered' groups. On the earliest known photographs of Papuans we find evidence of this use of cloth. As the anthropologist Nicholas Thomas has argued, the popularity of these objects as exchange items did not simply reflect a European commercial order of merit, say in it being cheap goods that could be 'forced' on the natives in exchange for something truly valuable.[12] The popularity of calico as an exchange good was also home-based in that local cultural traditions actually favoured an easy and successful appropriation of this lively coloured material.

Of course we should not forget there was another story as well. Under colonial rule wearing clothing was often forced on Papuans by colonial officers and missionaries zealously striving for what they regarded as civilised decency. As late as the 1980s women and girls in the remoter 'primitive' interior of New Guinea received pieces of cotton to be made and worn as bras for school and church. But this Western preoccupation with clothing as covering might not reflect the basic attraction that cloth had in itself, and still has for many Papuan groups. In New Guinea, clothing might indeed be quite different from cloth.

The introduction and adoption of T-shirts and other items of Western dress is of a more recent date than that of calico as such. With regard to T-shirts this is understandable. We already saw that their popularity in America and Europe was in itself a comparatively recent phenomenon. Moreover, prefabricated imported clothing was much more expensive than simple cloth by-the-yard and until recently it was less easily available outside the bigger towns on the island. Nevertheless even in the 1960s a few Asmat were already wearing shirts and pants, as can be seen on photographs taken by Gerbrands when he conducted his studies among this group. As elsewhere in New Guinea, much of this early use of Western dress probably was initiated by missionaries and anthropologists giving away second-hand clothing to helpful Papuans, as I myself did in the late seventies. In addition, government officers distributed shirts and pants to appointed village heads as a mark of their official status.

This explains an important difference in Papuan attitudes

towards cloth and clothing. Western clothing as it was distributed to the local population was much more closely associated with Western behaviour, style, and above all, power. Officials, missionaries and anthropologists – powerful and rich compared to the Papuans they governed, baptised and studied – were dressed in clothing that could only be read in terms of its owners' superior status. When I conducted my research, this difference in appreciation was clearly visible. The popular red calico I used as an exchange item in the village where I lived immediately entered a local circuit of use and meaning, being applied to a variety of local purposes. The shirts, trousers and boots that came their way, however, could not so easily be separated from their powerful Western image. Such clothing became the focus of a status wrangle between its owners and the other villagers, as it clearly signified the owner's close association with new centres of power and meaning. I once witnessed the strength of this symbolism when at a ceremonial dance one of the men chose to depict ' a Westerner' by borrowing shirts and trousers, painting himself completely white and as a final touch, fastening a pair of shoes on top of his head. His performance undoubtedly had an ironic edge, I fear at my expense as well, but this confirmed rather than diminished the powerful symbolism of the image.

Is this then what we see when looking at Roy Villevoye's parade of images and mannequins? Is this Asmat clothing simply an adoption of Western dress? If it is, it must perforce be an unsuccessful imitation because of the obvious mismatch between such symbols of power and prestige and the actual position of the Asmat who wear them. Its effect rather would be just the opposite. Such a borrowed image would only confirm the pitiable situation of these people in our and their own eyes. It would signify defeat, not only economic and political but also cultural. We would be right in our initial reaction to this display of torn, ragged and dirty shirts as a poverty parade.

To me, however, this is not what is happening here. It seems to me that Villevoye has captured something that is closely akin to our own adoption and transformation of what once was 'alien' and American. What is happening could perhaps best be described in the terms I used above: the Asmat, it seems, are turning clothing into cloth.

FROM RAGS TO RICHES
It is likely that the Asmat's first confrontation with European clothing was much the same as in the rest of New Guinea. The attraction of wearing such exotic attire – and thus being associated with the unknown world of the Europeans – must have been very great, if not irresistible. Perhaps Matjemosh, the woodcarver portrayed in Gerbrands' documentary about

the Asmat, got his shirt and shorts from him or from one of the missionaries. The few that owned such clothing stood out in the community, and they must have been proud of the special status it endowed them. These were treasured possessions no doubt, and even when dirty or in disrepair they retained their strong symbolic association with an alien and powerful world. The missionaries' drive towards Western notions of decency only confirmed this association in a different way as a new morality.

Yet since then a subtle change must have happened in Asmat attitudes toward this introduced dress code. When Roy Villevoye first visited the Asmat in 1992, the possession of Western clothing was no longer rare or exclusive. It clearly had become general. Judging from his earlier images, most men and women as well as children were wearing Western clothing of some sort. Of course the circumstances of their use – worn night and day while working in a tropical climate – are not favourable to a clean and pressed shirt. Tears are likely to occur. Throwing a torn shirt away to buy a new one is a Western consumer attitude which the Asmat can ill afford. So the shreds to some extent are signs of poverty.

But there is more to it than just poverty. The rags are their own and have a special significance. They have been turned into a stylistic asset. On what do I base this claim? On the fact that each dress seems to 'fit' the wearer in a special, individual way. Whatever we might think about the state of their dress, the wearers undoubtedly are at home in their personal attire. The ubiquity of its use indicates that this clothing no longer serves as a local marker of being closer to a powerful world far away. It suggests something else: the appropriation and transformation of Western clothing into a particular style of their own.

Looking at Villevoye's images from the perspective of cloth rather than clothing opens up alternative routes to understanding these new Asmat meanings of shirts. Let us make an inventory of what we see.

Actually the variety of body wear that Villevoye recorded is bewildering. Only a few shirts are comparatively clean and untorn. Most are dirty and discoloured to various degrees, with tears and holes and other unconventional irregularities. Others appear to us as a bundle of rags in the most literal sense, merely a collection of strings barely holding together. And then at the extreme end of fashion there are the virtual 'shirts'. It takes some close observation to notice people walking around with remnants that only vaguely suggest their origins as clothing, like a detached collar piece or a simple string of cloth. If we interpret all this as 'clothing' or even more general as 'covering', we are left with a riddle, or better: a credibility gap. We would have to suppose a serious misunderstanding – if not self-deception – on the part of the Asmat villagers were we to assume that even these unrecognisable remnants stand for covering in the conventional Western sense of the word.

There are in fact some clear pointers that guide us to a different interpretation. One such a pointer is that what the Asmat are doing is limited to upper body wear. The shorts and trousers they are wearing remain largely intact, apart from the wear and tear of daily life. There is no sign that these items have somehow been tampered with, customised or individualised by their owners. Shorts obviously have been adopted as a conventional modern dress of decency, much as in the Western world. The difference in attitude between these and the 'shirts' the Asmat are wearing is quite striking, and this strengthens our suspicion that there is something special going on with the upper part of their dress.

The second pointer is more intriguing. If we could see Villevoye's images in their sequence of time, like a story unfolding, we would notice that the rags become more and more elaborate and deliberate over time. The first footage of this movie would show shirts with accidental tears and rips. We would see torn shirts which are further embellished by their owners with apparently haphazard cuts. Gradually these cuts would become more deliberate and purposeful. And finally we would see some shirts appearing that are completely new and clean, yet cut to shreds in delicate patterns. It would dawn on us that what we are seeing are cuts of will rather than rags of fate.

The final pointer is both the most subtle and at the same time the most revealing. Most of the images and shirts that we are confronted with are worn by Asmat men. When Asmat women appear in Villevoye's photographs, however, we notice that when they wear a T-shirt it always is a second layer worn over a closed female dress. Like male shorts, this basic female dress surely conforms to the introduced Western convention of sexual decency. But the additional torn T-shirt on top of it is something else altogether. It must conform to something different, something which is not taken from Western convention or example but which refers to a notion that is truly local Asmat. The irony is that this local transformation in fact goes one step beyond the Western transformation. As we saw, the T-shirt originally was underwear and in the 1950s became popular as an outer garment. The Asmat women, however, have turned it into a bodice to be worn over the proper dress. The inside truly has become the outside.

THE ART OF THE LOWLY T-SHIRT

By now the identity of the Asmat T-shirt begins to emerge. Villevoye's images and installations are not renderings of the clothing fashions of the poor who cannot afford proper dress. We should stop thinking about them as T-shirts and start thinking about them as decorations, draperies perhaps, or embellishments. But then the next question is: embellishments of what? At this point we necessarily will have to venture into some anthropological speculation, which is not all that bad, because anthropology in itself always entails some – reasonable – speculation. Anthropology's basic assumption is, however, that any cultural endeavour always has some sort of logic. Culture is not a capricious conglomerate of customs and beliefs that falls apart when touched. The Asmat in particular do have a distinct cultural tradition that guides their perception of the world. Perhaps there is some way in which the transformations of supposedly superficial Western introductions like T-shirts can be understood as emanating from such existing perceptions.

The most obvious of these traditions is that of woodcarving. Museums like the Leiden Museum for Ethnography testify to the supreme importance of sculpture in the life of the Asmat. The symbolic significance of this aesthetic tradition is deeply anchored in Asmat culture, not only in the use and meaning of the sculptures themselves but also in the act of carving. Making sculpture is in many ways central to the self-image of Asmat men. It is precisely this tradition that may have some special relevance to the interpretation of the art of the lowly T-shirt.

There are several features of the Asmat sculptural tradition that draw our attention. There is the Asmat concern with the human and animal figure. The body clearly is a crucial element in Asmat aesthetics, not only as a stylistic form but also as the focus of a strong cultural symbolism. The second feature that seems significant is the elaborate *ajour* work that characterises some of the most important Asmat sculptures, such as the impressive ceremonial *bisj*-poles. Third, there is the tendency in Asmat woodcarving to formal abstraction in their symbolic representations. And finally there is yet another tradition – though apparently outside the realm of woodcarving – that should be mentioned. As can be seen in older photographs as well as in Villevoye's images, the Asmat often 'sculpt' their own bodies by means of scarification: deliberate (perhaps even accidental) wounds that are treated in such a way that they leave a visible and tangible ridge on the body.

If we put all this together a new picture emerges. It suggests that the Asmat use of T-shirts could be seen as emanating from a sculptural tradition focussed on the body as a central symbolic object. Or, more concretely: would it not make sense to interpret what the Asmat do with Western clothing as a new, alternative form of 'sculpting' with cloth, rather than as a pitiful attempt at clothing? Indeed, the images we see suggest that the concern of the Asmat is neither with covering nor with revealing. In that sense the Asmat rags are different from the former Western fashion of customising jeans by making deliberate cuts. Rather, the images suggest a primary concern with the body, as if the material of clothing gradually has been transformed into a new and malleable, sculptural skin.

This is all speculative, no doubt, and it would require an anthropologist to investigate whether there is some foundation for this interpretation. Yet I feel confident of at least one thing. What the Asmat do with these new and 'alien' things is not a misunderstanding, a mistake or the beginning of the end for a once authentic cultural tradition. It is our own guilty conscience that leads us to see the goods of industrial society that we take for granted as the root of all evil and the death of difference and authenticity. But when we look closely at our own history, we see that this is not necessarily true. We ourselves have transformed the T-shirt and blue jeans from an American icon into something that truly is our own. I am certain that with Villevoye's work we are witnessing the same process. We only have to clear our heads of the prejudice that Asmat and other non-Western societies should remain the living examples of an authenticity that we think we ourselves have lost.

THE ART OF COLLECTING

A journey to the islands of New Guinea, as in the days of Lesson, is still a singular and exciting experience. But today it is a very different journey. Nobody expects that the way of life of the people inhabiting the islands will be the same as in Lesson's time. Like everywhere else, New Guinea has been caught up in the web of modernisation. Urbanisation, money, politics, tourism and of course the material symbols of modernity such as planes, cars, motorcycles, radios and T-shirts have long since changed the life and the outlook of even the most isolated communities. So what we bring back from a contemporary journey, be it impressions, images or objects, will and should be different from those of previous times.

Lesson did bring back a great many things, ranging from unknown animal species to equally unknown exotic artefacts. His fear that these would disappear 'in that huge pit that we call a museum' undoubtedly has proved to be correct. We probably could track most of them down in the deep cellars of some Paris museum. His taxonomic way of exploring and collecting, something he would have found obvious and scientific, has long been discredited in anthropology. Of course, col-

lection is always a project of creating knowledge as well as a cultural (and personal) attitude. But knowledge does not necessarily have to be understood as analytic scientific knowledge. Rearranging the world in unexpected associative ways, ways that confront us with riddles instead of clear-cut answers, creates a different kind of knowledge of the human condition. In this sense, Villevoye's collection of shirts and images, even though it — like all collections — involves an ordering of some kind or another, is quite different from a traditional project of scientific taxonomy. It is a project of art that does not pretend to analyse or explain what it is we see.

Many modern artists prefer to regard their work as an alternative route to meaning and insight, a route that, if not actually opposed to science, certainly is inimical to it. Yet I think that the much maligned philosophers of the Enlightenment were certainly right in one respect. As the frontispiece of Diderot and d'Alembert's famous eighteenth-century *Encyclopédia* shows, they envisaged art and science (as well as religion) as stemming from the same fundamental source of inquiry about the human condition. To me this notion is basically right. Unfortunately, however, the Enlightenment philosophers saw such an inquiry mainly as a means of taming and conquering the world. Maybe we should therefore see this common source rather as a shared sense of deep wonder about the riddles of the world and our place in it.

Finally, let us not forget that there is at least one particular field in which art and science regularly touch. Many modern artists share a remarkable preoccupation with museum curators and numerous scientists: they are all avid collectors. In this respect Villevoye stands in a long tradition of artist-collectors. And it is this collecting that shows that the gulf is neither wide nor unbridgeable. Although an art project, it remained accessible to both ways of seeing. It is possible to appreciate art without mystifying our knowledge, just as it is possible to interpret the Asmat ways with rags without destroying the aesthetic experience.

NOTES

[1] 'The first accomplishment that one should study with all tribes whatever their civilisation is that of the kitchen.' P. Lesson, *Voyage autour du monde entrepris par ordre du gouvernement sur la corvette La Coquille*. Brussels 1839, vol. iv, p. 43 (my translation).

[2] 'The savage devours, half-civilised man eats, but only the very civilised human knows how to dine.' *Ibid.*, p. 29 (my translation).

[3] '… that vast pit, in France called museum, that like the vessel of the Danaïds receives constantly yet contains nothing.' *Ibid.*, p. 73 (my translation)

[4] A good introduction to the art of the Asmat can be found in Dirk Smidt (Ed.), *Asmat Art: Woodcarvings of Southwest New Guinea*. Amsterdam 1993. The frontispiece shows a spectacular row of *bisj*-poles.

[5] A.A. Gerbrands, *Wow-ipits. Eight Asmat Woodcarvers of New Guinea*. The Hague/Paris 1967; A.A. Gerbrands, *Matjemosh. A Woodcarver from the village of Amenamkai, Asmat Tribe on the Southwest Coast of New Guinea*. Utrecht 1963 (16 mm. movie).

[6] For some critical notes about the popular idea of the demise of authenticity through mass consumption see Nicholas Thomas, *In Oceania: Visions, Artifacts, Histories*. Durham/London 1997 (in particular p. 171 *ff*).

[7] For a short history and semiotics of the T-shirt as Western fashion see Betsy Cullum-Swan and Peter K. Manning, *What is a t-shirt? Codes, chronotypes and everyday objects*, in: Stephan Harold Riggins (Ed.), *The Socialness of Things*. Berlin/New York 1994, pp. 415-434. See also Eric de Kuyper, *De verbeelding van het mannelijke lichaam*, Nijmegen 1993.

[8] See also Daniel Miller, *Persons and blue jeans – Beyond fetishism*, in: Etnofoor, 3/1 1990.

[9] Respectively 'Yesus em i laip' (incorrect Pidgin, probably by a non-Papuan), 'Namba wan bia belong PNG' and 'Mi lukim yu bihain / me lukluk tasol'.

[10] See Paul Haenen, *Weefsels van wederkerigheid*. Nijmegen 1991 (diss.) and Jelle Miedema, *De Kebar 1855-1980*. Nijmegen 1984 (diss.).

[11] The quotation from Hondius van Herwerden at the beginning of this book gives a vivid illustration of the remarkable impact of red calico.

[12] Nicholas Thomas, *Entangled Objects: Exchange, Material Culture and Colonialism in the Pacific*

LITERATUUR

Betsy Cullum-Swan and Peter K. Manning, 'What is a t-shirt? Codes, chronotypes and everyday objects', in: Stephen Harold Riggins – THE SOCIALNESS OF THINGS – Berlin/New York 1994, p.415-434.

A.A. Gerbrands – MATJEMOSH. A WOODCARVER FROM THE VILLAGE OF AMENAMKAI, ASMAT TRIBE ON THE SOUTHWEST COAST OF NEW GUINEA – Utrecht 1963 (16 mm film).

A.A. Gerbrands – WOW-IPITS. EIGHT ASMAT WOODCARVERS OF NEW GUINEA – The Hague/Paris 1967

Paul Haenen – WEEFSELS VAN WEDERKERIGHEID – Nijmegen 1991 (thesis).

Eric de Kuyper – DE VERBEELDING VAN HET MANNELIJK LICHAAM – Nijmegen 1993.

P. Lesson – VOYAGE AUTOUR DU MONDE ENTREPRIS PAR ORDRE DU GOUVERNEMENT SUR LA CORVETTE LA COQUILLE – Brussels 1839.

Jelle Miedema – DE KEBAR 1855-1980 – Nijmegen 1984 (thesis).

Daniel Miller – PERSONS AND BLUE JEANS-BEYOND FETISHISM – in: Etnofoor, 3/1 1990.

Dirk Smidt (ed.) – ASMAT ART: WOODCARVINGS OF SOUTHWEST NEW GUINEA – Amsterdam 1993.

Nicholas Thomas – ENTANGLED OBJECTS: EXCHANGE, MATERIAL CULTURE AND COLONIALISM IN THE PACIFIC – Cambridge (Mass.) 1991.

AMALIA TOMAMNÁK, Pupis 1998

148

MARIA TONDAYIR, Er 2000

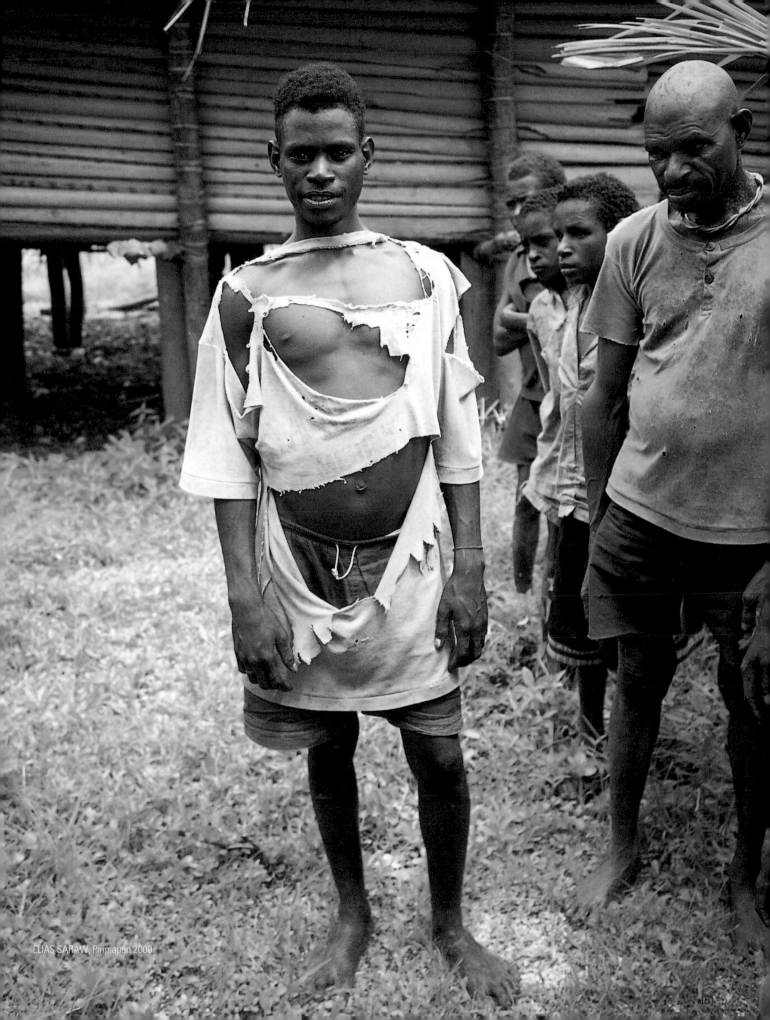

151

WATI VIMTAY, Er 2000

153

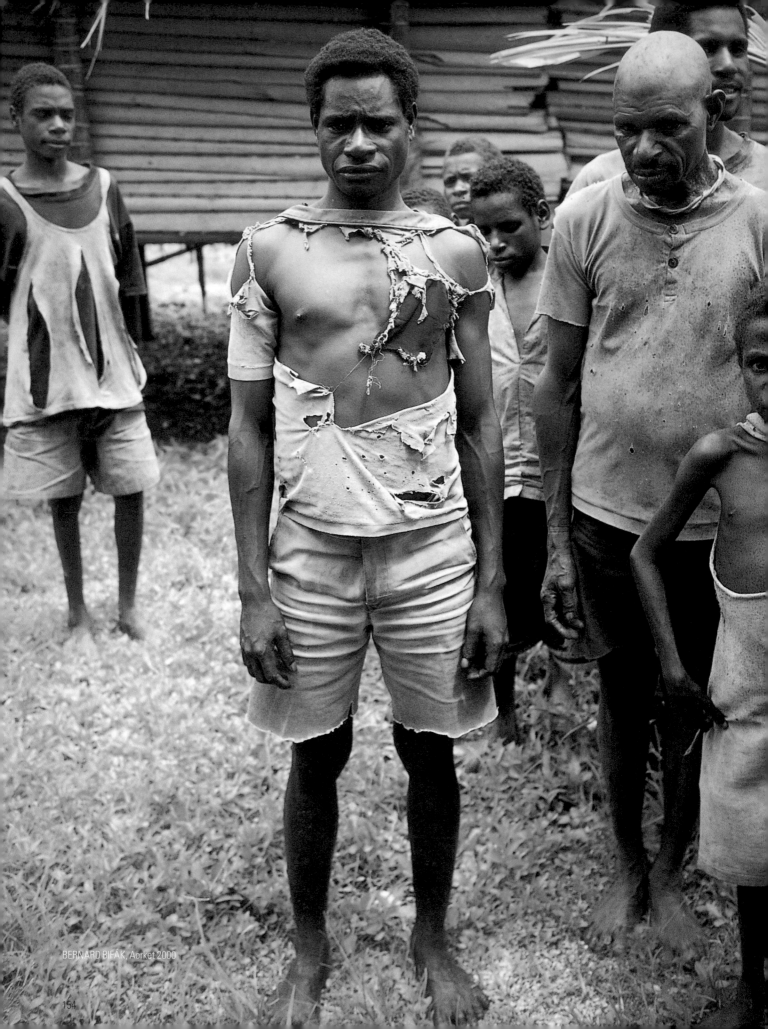

ANASTASIA KERAW, Aarket 2000

Sandra Niessen

THE PRISM OF FASHION: TEMPTATION, RESISTANCE AND TRADE

The history of colour follows the history of civilisation. Chenciner (2000: 29)

REVOLUTIONS IN COLOUR

In 'Pleasantville', a late nineties' Hollywood film, the characters and their surroundings are portrayed in black-and-white until they are willing to climb out of the set patterns of their calm, even naïve lives. Then they are enlivened by colour. Colour signifies their willingness to endorse life's complexity, experience emotion, be authentic. The film's director uses the viewer's innate longing for colour to solicit agreement with his perspective. Words with which we have grown up, 'colourless', 'drab', 'grey' and even 'beige' say it all: a world without colour is unbearable.

In the film, colour is given the role of the novel element, even though black-and-white is the real invention. We have never known black-and-white; we inhabit, inescapably, a world of colour, and the colours of nature have never been surpassed by synthetic invention or artistic rendition. We intuit that colour is as vital as the air we breathe. This may be why we so easily imagine that the kind of delight that must have attended the invention of synthetic colour in the 1850s must have been like the response to a brightened Hollywood screen. The invention of synthetic colour is billed as having allowed first Europe, and then the whole world, to exit a long, drab and monotonous age; there was a 'clamour for something new, something stunning', a 'hunger for different colours' (Beer 1959: 3).

To be sure, the invention of synthetic dyes was revolutionary in world history. The global ramifications – and they continue to be felt – are indisputable. Even the first industrially produced synthetic colour, *mauveine*, threw the fashions of Europe into a 'mauve decade'. And within ten years, synthetic dyes were altering the appearance of textiles around the world, to say nothing of how they altered patterns of thought, economics, production, politics, trade and social relations. Nevertheless the period after the invention of the first dyes is hardly comparable to a black-and-white Hollywood film after the addition of colour. The kinds of transformations sparked by the invention of synthetic dyes in the nineteenth century were, in fact, more the norm than the exception. For thousands of years the procurement of dyestuffs has led to social upheaval. Colour has been lusted after, and dyestuffs and polychrome cloth have been traded across tremendous distances, for as long as we have records to consult. Moreover, textile dyes at the time of the invention of synthetic dyes were more accessible in northern Europe than at any previous time in her history.

The current era is heralded as having global fashion. It is a heady time in which fashions are inspired by the clothing of every culture and invented (so it seems) by designers of every nationality. Design reference is unlimited, subject to will. Choice is infinite, unencumbered; authenticity is a non-issue; the creative licence of the designer is everything. During the ArtEZ symposium Global Fashion / Local Tradition that launched the production of the present volume, a group of talented students from the Textile and Fashion Department of the Royal Academy for Visual Arts in The Hague held a fashion show on the theme of Folklore.[2] They strutted their borrowings and interpretations of the clothing of indigenous peoples from China, the Caucasus, Tibet, the Philippines and other corners of the globe (fig. 1) in harmonious counterpoint, with discussions about fashion inventions by Galliano, Gaultier, Xuly Bët, Chalayan and other global-age designers (see José Teunissen this volume).

Seduced by the multicultural images, we may be prone to a skewed historicism and blind to fashion's unprecedented imperialism. Scholars have argued that a typically Western view of the world (or ego) emerged coincident with Western industrial dominance, beginning with the textile trade. Humbler days, when Europeans struggled to be competitive in the global networks of trade for dyestuffs and colourful cloth, are too quickly, perhaps too conveniently, forgotten. Fashion's ethnic novelties generate a false sense that the global, multicultural nature of fashion is unprecedented. Fashion globalisation is ego-stroking.

The history of trade in textile dyestuffs is a tale that has taken place in every corner of the globe for hundreds of years. It provides a unique lens through which to observe the phenomenon of fashion. The bird's-eye thumbnail sketch that I provide below of revolutionary moments of change in the colours of European fashion demonstrates that historically, local choices about what to wear may have correlated with macro-developments in the production and trade of dyestuffs.

Focussing a little more closely through the historical lens, we appear to be approaching the end of a colour revolution. Only decades ago, synthetic dyestuffs started to be produced 'offshore'. Now, in 2005, the East is on the brink of once again becoming the largest producer and consumer of textiles and textile dyes. For more than a millennium India clothed the world, and China was the main supplier of silk. Three hundred years ago, Europe did not have the know-how in dyeing and printing textiles, nor sufficient access to quality dyestuffs, to be able to compete with India. And competition had to be on the terms of the standard-setter. The kick-start inventions of the industrial revolution – the fly shuttle in 1733, the spinning jenny in 1764 and the power loom in 1785 – allowed England to wrest global dominance in the textile trade out of the hands of the East. Around the same time, Europe was making huge

above: Map
under: FOLKLORE FASHION SHOW put on by the Royal Academy of the Visual Arts, The Hague,
at the conference on GLOBAL FASHION / LOCAL TRADITION held in Arnhem, 28 January 2005.

advancements in her printing and dyeing techniques, and when synthetic dyes were invented 150 years ago, it gave Europe and England independence from the suppliers of natural dye materials. A global fate was sealed. It became the turn of the East to learn to compete on the terms set by the West.

EARLY TRADE IN COLOUR:
WHEN INDIA CLOTHED THE WORLD

India was able to 'clothe the world' because she possessed the winning combination of textile features known at the time. She specialised in cotton fabrics that were well-woven, lightweight and cool; they were decorated with diverse and sophisticated patterning; the bright colours didn't run or fade in the light and during washings. Her ability to meet the design requirements of her trading partners also facilitated her dominance. That skilled workers needed to fill orders accurately was something that European trading companies who tried to win a role in the Indian textile trade were to learn quickly when the wrong stripe, pattern or colour tone meant a considerable financial loss (Anderson 1971 [1826]).

India was supplying cloth directly and indirectly to the Far East, Central Asia, Southeast Asia, the Arab world, the Mediterranean and Africa, as well as to home markets in the South Asian continent, when the tardy northern Europeans joined in the Asian trade network. One of the greatest trade networks in world history, extending from the Mediterranean in the West to China in the East, had been in existence since the first century B.C. Goods were relayed in both directions overland and by sea. Until its fall, the Roman Empire constituted the western pole. From the sixth to the eleventh centuries, the capital shifted to Byzantium. Indian cloth entered at various points along the trajectory.

Tang China, the eastern pole, was strongly oriented towards things foreign and hosted visitors from East and West Asia and the Middle East. Her wealth expanded on the strength of her trade ties with India as well as Central and Southeast Asia. And China supplied silk. This wonderful fabric constituted 90 percent of the goods entering the West. The material was discovered in China in around 2000 B.C. and only gradually spread westward, so that China enjoyed a monopoly of long duration. The fibre is important to any discussion of colour in textiles because the long, smooth filaments reflect light evenly, producing a lustrous sheen. To be sure, it wasn't just the silk fibre that inspired such longing; it was what silk did for colour. Cloth is a delicate, perishable material. Despite its importance in early trade, it is rare to find tangible evidence of that importance. One of the earliest is a piece of bright blue Chinese silk from the necropolis of Al Azam, Egypt. It dates

from between the late thirteenth and early fourteenth centuries (Vollmer et al. 1983: 18).

In addition to links with China, India hooked into the East-West trade along the Silk Road at the western pole by way of the Red Sea, the Arab world by way of the Persian Gulf and Central Asia by way of an arduous overland route. According to Arabic, Chinese and European sources, colourful cloth was one of western India's important trade goods from as early as the first century A.D. (Guy 1998: 41). The trade must have been considerable and the desire for the goods great because Pliny complained that the purchase of Indian cottons was impoverishing Rome. Silks were also among the goods traded by India, but she had to compete with production in Iraq, Iran and China. Findings of red and blue cotton fragments from Gujarat in Fostat, Egypt, near the Red Sea (see map), date from the ninth to the seventeenth centuries. Chequered cotton finds from the Tellem caves of North Africa dating from the eleventh century likely came from India. The earliest finds reveal that India was familiar with blue (indigo) and red (madder, chay, brazilwood) dyes, as well as resist dyeing techniques.

In an eastward direction, India's trade influence extended into both mainland and insular Southeast Asia. The climate there is not conducive to the preservation of cloth, but the careful storage of old trade cloth from India by many tribal peoples of Southeast Asia is ample evidence of the high esteem in which it was, and still is, held. Srivijaya, the ancient Sumatran polity that controlled the traffic through the Strait of Malacca, thrived on its intermediate position between India to the west, China to the east, and its strategic proximity to mainland Southeast Asia to the north. It is likely that knowledge of dyestuffs and other techniques was part of the exchange, the opportunity presenting itself because Indian traders established trading settlements along their routes.

It may be assumed that India was developing a skill at producing according to the taste of her many and varied markets. John Guy's (1998) hypothesis that, given the two-way flow of ideas and goods, India's entire sphere of trade influence constituted a design melting pot, seems plausible enough. It is precisely this kind of design exchange in the twenty first century fashion world that is stirring up so much excitement, the only difference being the unprecedented speed at which that exchange is now taking place as a result of mechanised production and telecommunications.

India's design melting pot extended all the way up to the Mediterranean, which was therefore richly endowed with the highest quality dyestuffs from tropical regions as well as polychrome and luxury textiles. By the thirteenth century, Italy had learned the secret of silk production. Ancient trade paths led from the Mediterranean across the Sahara into West Africa, along which large quantities of luxury goods including cotton, silk and wool as well as dyestuffs were transported (Gilfoy 1987: 18-25). It is likely that both Chinese and Indian cloth figured in that trade. The trade became the underpinnings of the great empire of Ghana.

To the north, Flanders became the textile capital of northern Europe, known for its proficiency at dyeing wool with a mixture made from the locally grown woad and madder. For polychrome products, northern Europe sent its cloth to dyers in Italy, the leader in polychrome dyeing for all of Europe. The quality of the Italian products was of such importance in the fifteenth century that the use of inferior dyes (such as woad and madder) was prohibited by law. Trade did occur, in other words, between northern Europe and the Mediterranean despite the barrier formed by the Alps, and northern Europe did have access to quality dyes from the tropics. However, the only thing of real value in northern Europe to exchange for them was precious metals. According to Schneider (1978) the darker colours worn in northern Europe, especially black, were not just symptomatic of restricted access to colourful dyestuffs but also of restraint.[3] Polychrome luxury cloths and dyestuffs from the south were 'tempting but ruinous' because they would drain the north of its gold. The ascetic mores of medieval Christianity facilitated the economic boycott of luxury goods. Black became a sign of devotion and bright colours of questionable morals and unbridled consumption. The resistance to colour in northern Europe encouraged the development of the local textile industry, and thus political and economic autonomy.

CIRCUMNAVIGATING THE GLOBE WITH DYESTUFFS
Patterns of world trade began to shift as a result of technological advancements in northern Europe. The notion that the world is round gained credence in the fifteenth century, and circumnavigation of the world followed in the second decade of the sixteenth century. In his attempt to discover the East by going west, Columbus set foot on the New World in 1492 and claimed it for Spain. Portugal sailed directly to the East by way of Africa and quickly built trade ties with South and Southeast Asia. Capturing the island of Hormuz in the Persian Gulf, she was able to control the trade to Syria and Turkey; settling at Goa on the west coast of India, she gained access to Indian cottons and silks; capturing Malacca, she was in control of the trade between India and China and all of Southeast Asia; settling at Macao, she had access to Chinese goods. The trade dominance of Spain and Portugal was broken by England toward the end of the sixteenth century, when

Captain Francis Drake plundered Spanish possessions and eventually destroyed the Spanish Armada. The Dutch shook off the Portuguese and Spanish monopoly in the Asian spice trade at the end of the century by sending their own fleet to the East Indies and taking control of strategic Portuguese bases. By discovering sea routes to the East, northern Europe succeeded in breaking the ancient patterns of East-West trade, bypassing the controlling Levantine gateway of the Mediterranean (Byzantium had fallen into Turkish hands in 1453) and avoiding Italian monopolies in the luxury trade. In 1600 the British set up the East India Company to facilitate direct trade with the East, and two years later the Dutch set up their own Dutch East India Company. The 1600s mark the beginning of European colonisation.

With respect to textiles and dyes, the European textile printing industry was at a low point in the sixteenth century. In the fifteenth century, textiles were printed with black ink by book printers in the same way that books were printed. Blue and red attracted the interest of the industry during the course of the seventeenth century. During that century the influx and use of colour in northern Europe was symptomatic of new long-distance trade relations and easier and cheaper access to high quality dyestuffs.

Dyestuffs were eagerly sought after in those days and were among the first cargoes to be brought back by the voyages to the East. Indigo had reached the Mediterranean from India by way of the Red Sea since the Middle Ages, but that access made it too expensive to replace the inferior but locally-grown woad (Smit 1928:109). When Portugal began trading directly by sea with Asia, however, shiploads of the blue dye reached northern Europe. At first, woad cultivators would have nothing of it, and those who had a great deal invested in the trade in woad fiercely resisted its importation. 'On the continent, the resistance to the use of indigo sometimes took dramatic forms. Expulsion from the city, high fines and threats to cut off the right hand appear in many sentences.'[4] (Hofenk de Graaff 1985: 28) In the end, indigo prevailed. It was a better and cheaper dyestuff. Spain set up indigo plantations especially in the West Indian colonies of Guatemala and Caracas; the French and British had followed suit in their own colonies by the middle of the seventeenth century.

The Spanish also began to import cochineal or 'Spanish Red' from New Spain. Much admired for its vivid colour, it partly displaced the brazil wood that Europe had obtained from the East in the Middle Ages (and later from American coasts) (Donkin 1977: 7), and eventually kermes, another insect dye known since ancient times by the Romans and extensively traded throughout Europe, Persia, India, and China. The

Spanish encouraged the cultivation of cochineal in Mexico and Guatemala, and later from Ecuador to Peru. Its trade value was described as 'almost equal to silver' (Donkin 1977: 25, 37). Because Spain held a monopoly on the cochineal trade, the material entered Europe through Spain or the Netherlands (which was politically linked to Spain). Arriving in Venice, it entered the intercontinental trade involving Constantinople, the Levant and western Asia. Ships of the English East India Company carried it directly to India – although it never replaced the Indian lac dye. It eventually reached China in the eighteenth century, carried by Spanish ships to the Philippines (Donkin 1977: 38).

Brazil wood, formerly available only from India, yielded a clear, red colour and could now be imported from Brazil. Prized for its deep, black colour, logwood was obtained from the eastern shores of Central America.

In other words, each of the popular, high-quality tropical dyestuffs exemplifies early international trade. Furthermore, the skills required to deploy those dyes came from international sources. Flemish, German and Portuguese dyers were brought in to teach their skills in the north, thereby weaving still more densely the international threads of the dye and textile industry. Dyeing was a complex craft – as anyone who has ever worked with natural dyes knows – and dyers were held in high esteem for their abilities. Under their tutelage, the use of polychrome in textiles spread like an ink-blot from France and Germany into England and Holland. Success encouraged more experimentation with dye recipes and expansion of the local cultivation of woad, saffron and madder.

REVOLUTIONS OF RISING COLOUR EXPECTATIONS

Given the great advancements made by European manufacturers in the textile industry and their growing need for markets, early involvement in the Asian trade networks must have been a great disappointment because it quickly became apparent that the quality of English and Dutch woollens was still too low to compete with Indian cloth. It was not enough for European goods to be desirable in the East as a novelty. Indian cottons, on the other hand, sustained the trade throughout the East and were indispensable commodities of exchange for other products that the Europeans desired, such as spices. Although the Europeans were not able to use their own textiles in this trade, their shipping competence gave them an important edge. They were able to take goods from India more quickly and cheaply to North Africa, Turkey and the Levant by sea than the earlier practice of exporting them through the Red Sea or the Persian Gulf, and then overland by expensive caravan traffic (Irwin and Schwartz 1966:11), another illustration of how the global web that had been spun for more than a millennium and a half by the coloured cloth of India became denser and more extensive through European involvement.

Initially, Indian cloth was also little more than a novelty in England and Holland, the reason also having to do with colour application. Indian patterning did not appeal to European taste. Anxious to stimulate a home market, the trade companies began to commission works by supplying samples of European designs for Indian dyers and printers to copy. The strategy worked. Within decades European demand for Indian goods was overwhelming (Irwin and Schwartz 1966: 44- 45) to the extent that consumers were willing to bleed their countries of the gold necessary to procure those goods rather than to forego them – a situation reminiscent of Pliny's concern for the health of the Roman economy more than a millennium before, and the resistance of northern Europe to southern polychrome luxuries prior to the discovery of the sea routes to Asia. The solution of re-trade took on new urgency as a way to recoup some of the gold that was being lost in the original procurement.[5]

The East India Company policy of commissioning textile designs compatible with English tastes encouraged the development of exotic, multicultural design mixtures. The English designs were 'modified in Indian hands, and then the Indianised versions were welcomed as new and exotic back again in Europe' (Irwin and Schwartz 1966: 53). The design exchange became that much more complex because the English had become enamoured of Chinese patterning at the end of the seventeenth century and had developed their own forms of *chinoiserie*. These were among the samples sent to India, such that an Indian form of *chinoiserie* emerged. 'At the final stage we find Indian *chinoiserie* designs being sent from Madras to Canton for copying by Chinese embroiderers and silk-painters. By this time it was a convention so far removed from authentic Chinese art that Cantonese embroiderers were probably unaware of its Chinese origins at all.' (Irwin and Schwartz 1966:53) (fig. 3a) England had been drawn into the Asian fold of reciprocal multicultural design influences.

The popularity of Indian chintz, which reached its peak in Europe in 1685, had to do – in great measure – with colour. 'These cloths acquire their value and price from their brightness and, if I may say so, from the solidity and fastness of the colours they are dyed with, and which, far from losing their brilliance by washing, actually grow more beautiful' (Father Coeurdoux, missionary to India, and famous for his description of indigenous dyeing techniques, cited in Irwin 1966: 104). They were used by rich and poor alike in all manner and form: as fancy dress and sleepwear, outerwear and linings,

upper left: BONNET, 1760-1780, India. Nederlands Openluchtmuseum, Arnhem. Caption: Chintz from the Coromandel Coast in southeast India lines this straw bonnet. It was worn in the Zaan region of the Netherlands. / upper right: MORNING GOWN, mid-eighteenth century, northwest India. Rijksmuseum Amsterdam. This coat was inspired by Japanese robes. The Dutch East India Company ordered most from the southeast coast of India, although the name suggests northwest India. Made of oriental fabrics, the Indian patterning was probably painted in India. Such coats were generally worn indoors.

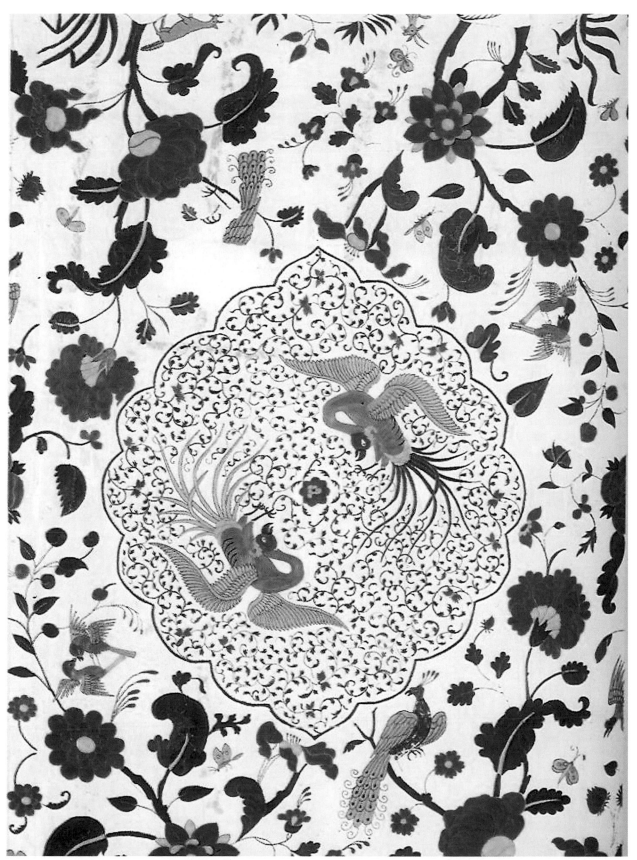

right page under: Reconstruction of a CHAMBER AT SCHLOSSHOF, Austria, 1725. Bundessammlung alter Stilmöbel Wien. Caption: Chintz became very popular in interior décor.
left page: Detail of a central fragment of a COVERLET with silk embroidery on cotton tabby ground, late 17th century, India. Royal Ontario Museum. (from Vollmer, p. 122).
This coverlet illustrates the multi-cultural influences in the textiles made in India for the English market. The coverlet depicts flowering trees, phoenixes, foxes, and peacocks.

wall-coverings and upholstery fabric. The heavily laden VOC ships that docked at Amsterdam, the European centre of re-distribution, couldn't keep up with the European demand.

The consequences of the calico craze were considerable. In panic, first England and then France and other European countries passed sumptuary laws in an attempt to bridle the demands of fashion that were threatening the domestic woollen industry. But resistance proved to be in vain. The strategy chosen by the Dutch, and eventually followed in Germany, France, England, Spain and Switzerland, was to revive their own languishing textile printing industry by adapting and applying Indian printing methods. There is evidence that the new printing strategies actually came from 'Turks' (or Armenians) who immigrated to the Netherlands. Coming from places situated half-way between East and West, they had knowledge of the Indian techniques (Smit 1928). The first new-style printing industry in Amsterdam was set up in 1678.

The Indian printing technique involved the use of mordants in combination with madder. Coffee brown, gold brown, light and dark red, and purple were all derived from madder, depending on the mordant used, and none faded in sunlight or ran when washed. As in India, carved wooden blocks were used to apply the mordants to the cloth so that the dyes would take in patterns. Indigo does not require working with mordants. To apply this blue dye in patterns, resist techniques were used. A wax-like substance was applied to the cloth in the areas that were to be left undyed, so that they would not take up the dye when the cloth was submerged in the dye vat.

The processes were slow and complicated, requiring a large amount of start-up capital, much inside and outside space, considerable personnel, expert knowledge and experience, and a wide range of ingredients including access to clean, flowing water. But the effort and risk were worth it. By the middle of the eighteenth century there were claims that the Dutch imitations could scarcely be distinguished from the Indian originals (Smit 1928: 64). Dyeing techniques were guarded in secrecy to thwart the rapidly emerging competition.

The success of the new enterprise increased the demand for dyestuffs. Tropical dyes came from the colonies. In addition, the cultivation of madder expanded considerably in France, Sweden, Denmark and England, eventually breaking the centuries-old Dutch monopoly. More cotton cloth was imported from India until mechanised spinning and weaving processes changed that into a demand for raw cotton.

NORTHERN EUROPEAN POLYCHROMES GO MULTI-NATIONAL

Northern Europe was able to flood Italy's markets with cheaper imitations of its own polychrome wares, thereby undercutting Italian production and capturing dominance of the European textile markets from which it had been excluded – or from which it had withdrawn, sheltering its industry and independence behind a black protectionist shield. This inversion in textile production dominance was paralleled by a remarkable flip-flop in European fashions. The north was now less restrained in the use of polychrome fabric, foregoing some preference for black. In economic self-defence, the Italians wrote sumptuary legislation against the 'gaudy and outlandish' northern products – and began wearing the black with which we are currently familiar in southern Europe (Schneider 1978: 436). The European code of colour had been reversed. Now it was Italy's turn to try to learn the techniques developed in Holland and England to try to compete in the textile industry.

On a wider geographical scale, something comparable occurred between northern Europe and India. India was hit not only by Europe's ability to copy her textile printing techniques, but by the mechanised spinning and weaving tools of the industrial revolution. Eventually, Europe was able to meet the Asian demand for cloth so skilfully and cheaply that it undercut Indian production. After 1820, the manufacture of Indian cotton textiles declined steadily (Bean 1989: 361). By 1825, two centuries after the earliest direct shipments of chintz to England and Holland, hand-spinning in India had virtually died out. From the greatest exporter of coloured cottons to the world, India had become one of the greatest importers of both yarn and fabrics.

The global web of trade woven around Indian textile production shifted as a result of the competition from European production. It is possible to point to the emergence of several new multicultural crucibles of design influence, but I restrict myself here to describing one that was catalysed by Dutch involvement. It relates to the technique of batik, an ancient strategy for applying colour to cloth that the Dutch encountered on Java. While the origins of batik on Java are unclear, what is certain is that the technique is one of the oldest in the world and that it achieved a zenith of perfection on Java. Different styles and technical variations were found throughout the island, reflecting different regional and historical circumstances.

When the Dutch East India Company (the VOC), which had wrested monopoly from India and other European competitors, went bankrupt towards the end of the eighteenth century, places that had traded for centuries with India were left without the regular supply of trade cloth to which they had grown accustomed. Another style of batik developed on Java's North Coast to fill some of the gap and was soon traded throughout the archipelago. Easily recognised for its abundant, bright colours, its designs reflected the mixture of indigenous Javanese, Chinese and European influences that were found on the North Coast as a result of the colonial presence (figs. 4b and c). The batik production workshops in the new style were the initiative of Indo-Europeans.

Back in the Netherlands, the eighteenth-century textile printing industry attempted to imitate batik in order to corner the Javanese market. While the results were not hugely popular, most buyers were of mixed descent: Javanese, European, Chinese and Arab. In time, the Dutch were also making imitations of the new North Coast batik styles (fig. 4d). The reciprocal design influence between European mechanical production and the wax-drawn production on Java is reminiscent of the back-and-forth blending of English and Asian design ideas when the East India Company commissioned calicoes a century earlier.

Always on the lookout for new markets, the Dutch tried to sell their batik prints in West Africa. In the days of the VOC, the Dutch had participated in the trade of Indian guinea cloth to West Africa. This was a very ancient trade tie indeed, if one counts the indirect trade of Indian goods over the Sahara from the Mediterranean. As Europe and Britain experimented with printing strategies to compete with Indian cloth, Africa was one of the markets that they tried to conquer. Success was a result of their ability to cater to minute regional differences in African taste, just as their Indian predecessors had been able to do. West African taste had been primed for batik by West African soldiers who had served in Indonesia (1810-1862) and brought batik back with them as gifts, and also by Dutch traders who had put in at African ports on their way back to Holland from Java with batik to exchange for food. In the second half of the nineteenth century, the Dutch began to produce so-called wax-prints specifically for the African market (Nielsen 1974). At the beginning of the twentieth century, when Indonesia took measures to protect its domestic batik production, Africa became the exclusive market for the Dutch batik. Ironically, the 'real (i.e. Dutch-made) thing' has become a deeply-rooted African status symbol, even though none of the designers of the fabrics is African. Local African textile producers find themselves in the curious position of having to copy the so-called Veritable Wax Hollandais in order to corner a share of the local market.

When the slave era ended, many of the Javanese peasants that the Dutch had brought to the West Indies to work on the plantations (1895-1939) ended up staying. Yet another batik design variant developed in Surinam as a result (about which still far too little is known).

SYNTHETIC DYES ENTER THE TRADE
The first synthetic dye, a purple colour, began to be industrially produced in 1857. The inventor, an Englishman named William Perkin, received little support for his initiative; there was simply too little general interest in applying his new invention.[6] Queen Victoria gave the industry the jump-start it needed in 1858 when she wore a gown dyed with Perkins's invention to her eldest daughter's wedding. Her endorsement launched a rage (fig. 5). New colours were invented in rapid succession, each snatched up in turn and pulled into the fashion parade.

Around the world, even in isolated places, endorsement of the new dyes was rapid, mainly because of the time they saved (up to years for a single dye lot) and their ease of use. To cite but one example, indigenous Guatemalan weavers used them, according to one analysis, 'almost immediately'. Their handwovens have become almost synonymous with sizzling bright colours, largely derived from synthetic dyes. Alizarin red was patented in England and Germany in 1871, and during the period 1875-1927 all Guatemalan textiles embellished with red were dyed with alizarin. Prior to that time, red appeared only rarely in Guatemalan cloth (Carlsen and Wenger 1991: 369).[7] Even India became an importer of synthetic colours.

The natural dye industry collapsed, whereupon whole segments of international trade crumbled and Europe settled comfortably into a period of dyestuff self-sufficiency. Cochineal was one of the first victims. In the 1860s, at the height of its popularity, the industry was 'fatally crippled' by the availability of synthetic dyes (Donkin 1977: 31). Although madder was synthesised in 1868, the production of 'Turkey red' didn't reach its peak until 1898. By then, 'madder was cultivated throughout the world. In Europe madder was grown in France particularly in the south and Alsace, Holland, Germany in Silesia, Saxony, Palatinate, Bavaria and Baden, Belgium, Austro-Hungary, Italy particularly in Tuscany; Naples and Sicily, Spain and Boeotia in Greece. In southern Russia cultivation flourished in the Caucasus and along the Caspian coast and in Kazan. Outside Europe madder was grown in Turkey, particularly Asia Minor, Persia, Mesopotamia, North Africa — Egypt, Algiers, Tunis, Tripoli and Morocco, Terceira on the Azores, North, South and Central America, the East Indies and Australia.' (Chenciner 2000: 82)

above: BATIK in the style of the North Coast of Java showing colonial influence
under: Detail. Colourful BATIK in the style of the North Coast of Java. Collection S. Niessen
The bright colouring inspired by the Chinese colour palette was facilitated by synthetic dyes.

above: VERITABLE WAX HOLLANDAIS, a so-called Dutch wax-print made for the West African market.

under: HEADCLOTH (angisa), Suriname. Prior to 1963, Suriname. Tropenmuseum, Amsterdam. A Suriname batik style emerged through the presence of Javanese labourers brought in by the Dutch to work on the plantations. The angisa was part of an outfit also including a skirt (koto) and jacket (jaki), worn on special occasions. above: Detail. Batik in the style of the North Coast of Java showing colonial influence.

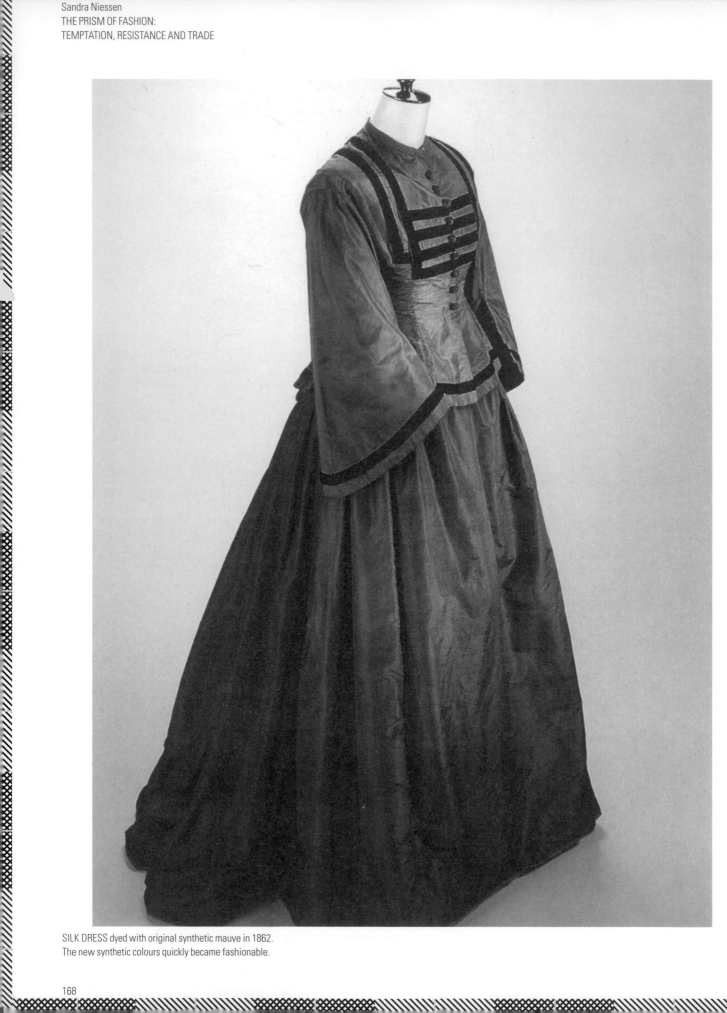

SILK DRESS dyed with original synthetic mauve in 1862.
The new synthetic colours quickly became fashionable.

The initial resilience of the dye may be attributed to the enormous growth in the textile printing industry in northern Europe. Demise followed in 1936 upon the development of naphtol dyes. The immediate effect was starvation among the French peasant cultivators. Within ten years, madder was abandoned nearly everywhere (Chenciner 2000:83).

Indigo, the other important dyestuff used in the production of calicoes, had become a major crop in European colonies throughout the tropics. A. von Bayer synthesised the dyestuff in 1878, and in 1897 BASF brought it onto the market. The statistics are revealing: in 1895-96, India exported 18,700 tons of indigo, and Germany imported natural indigo at a value of 20 million marks; by 1913-14, India's indigo export had shrunk to a mere 1,000 tons, while Germany's export of synthetic indigo was more than 50 million marks (Sandberg 1989: 35).

Less obvious than the cessation of international natural dyestuff cargoes to Europe was the challenge to indigenous systems presented by the synthetic dyestuffs that were traded in the opposite direction. Throughout the world, colours in indigenous societies were imbued with local meanings. Among a range of other things, colours commonly were associated with the compass points. Heringa (1989) has described how, in the Tuban region of northern Java, the colours marking the compass points also symbolised the stages of the human life cycle, thereby imparting meaning to what people wore as well as to how cloth was dyed. Colours, in other words, bridged conceptions of time and space, individual and society, and this symbolism informed the daily handling of cloth and dyes. While there was a tendency on the part of indigenous peoples, at least initially, to use synthetic colours as replacements of the locally available natural colours, the new colours presented an undeniable challenge, even linguistically: how should they be named? And how must they be accommodated within the people's worldview?[8] Dyestuffs available in boxes and bottles from the shop rather than from plants, insects, soils and types of water initiated a separation between colour and the immediate environment, a loosening from indigenous meaning systems. European-influenced batik produced on northern Java initially showed a livelier colour palette than elsewhere on Java because of the influence of the Chinese system of colour classification. This was augmented by the introduction of synthetic dyes. Certainly the new dyes were immediately endorsed because of their ease of use, proving to be a considerable time-saving measure. But they also introduced a new market/currency dependency. It is clear from the increased use of a more varied colour palette in indigenous handicrafts around the world that the availability of the rainbow of synthetic colours encouraged a departure from indigenous systems of colour classification,

and introduced colour as an arbitrary factor of individual taste. Again, colour took on the characteristics of exuberance and daring, with an unequalled capacity to break sacred and ancient cultural codes.

The first colour inventions were imperfect and in many cases inferior to their natural predecessors. Production often involved toxic chemicals for which no controls and standards of use had yet been developed. Furthermore, the colours were not always fast, to the disappointment of consumers. Nevertheless, synthetic dyes became indispensable to the clothing industry within a matter of decades. The tremendous growth in the domestic textile industry during the nineteenth century worked in their favour. Between 1851 and 1857 alone, calico exports increased fourfold and employment in the silk industry doubled (Garfield 2000: 44, 45). Regardless of the failings of synthetic dyes, the demand for textile colouring had surpassed any ability to return to natural dyes.

It is not surprising that some reactions to the new dyes were negative. In 1900, the Shah of Persia prohibited the use of aniline dyes for rugs because of their fugitive and inferior quality. He had the dyes seized and publicly burned, the users fined and jailed (Garfield 2000: 103).

The brightness of the dyes disturbed others. A French visitor to Hyde Park in 1862 commented derisively on the 'glare' of the dresses coloured with synthetic dyes (Garfield 2000: 77, 78; Ribeiro 1986: 130-131). In the summer of 1884 there appears to have been an aversion to brilliant colours, with the *Daily News* characterising fashionable dress as having 'no violent contrasts, no rude tints, all is soft and harmonious' (Newton 1974: 86). Aniline dyed clothing, it appeared, like face paint and dyed hair, could cast the virtue of its wearer into doubt (Ribeiro 1986: 130). Artifice, colour, opulence and seduction were apparently mixed in the same conceptual pot.

A practical reason for rejecting synthetic colour was related to the health of the wearer. In France and Switzerland arsenic acid was one of the ingredients in the early fuchsine dye, causing a serious threat when it leaked into the ground water (Garfield 2002: 89, 101-103). Arsenic residue on dyed textiles was harmful when wet. Dr Jaeger, a leader in London's health reform movement at the time of the 1884 International Health Exhibition, advised people to wear undyed materials in the summer, pointing out that dyed materials were 'least injurious in winter, in cold climates, when the body is in repose, and for Sunday visiting…' (cited in Newton 1974: 102). Skin diseases resulted from wearing aniline dyed fabrics next to the skin even if no arsenic was involved. Death, illness, court cases, closed and ruined factories all followed in the wake of the

INDIGENOUS SASHES, Guatemala. Collection S. Niessen.
Guatemalan Indians began to use synthetic colours 'immediately' after they were invented.
Guatemalan embroidery is now almost synonymous with sizzling, bright colours.

large-scale production of synthetic dyes.

At the end of the nineteenth century, the artist William Morris, the foremost spokesman of a craft revival movement in England, didn't hide his distaste for synthetic dyes (although he did use some of them): 'Anyone wanting to produce dyed textiles with any artistic quality in them must entirely forego the modern and commercial methods in favour of those which are at least as old as Pliny, who speaks of them as being old in his time.... These colours in fading remain beautiful, and never, even after long wear, pass into nothingness, through that stage of livid ugliness which distinguishes the commercial dyes as nuisances, even more than their short and no means merry life.' (cited in Chenciner 2000: 271)

The same aversion to the mechanical age was mirrored in the response of a group of Dutch artists in the same period who elected to express themselves using the batik technique, even while Dutch industrialists were lucratively engaged in selling batik prints to Africa. 'The underlying philosophy of the revival of European crafts, which rejected the industrial, mass-produced objects and perceived the process of their production as a lifeless automatic procedure, required that all utilitarian objects should be the outcome of unique creative processes, embedded with artistic qualities and representing high standards of workmanship.... Javanese batik textiles offered European artists the technical qualities they most admired: hand-applied wax-resist provided each of the decorated fabrics with individual, unique features resulting from the touch of the human hand and allowed a great degree of personal expression.' (Wronska-Friend 2001:107)

The most sublime Dutch examples were made by Chris Lebeau and his student, Berta Bake. Clearly, natural dye recipes had already been forgotten because the artists worked closely with the Colonial Museum in Haarlem to develop ones appropriate to their work. Synthetic dyes and the mechanised print industry had very quickly demoted what had once been conceived of as 'industry' on Java to 'handicraft' and 'art'. The Dutch works (rather than the 'original' Javanese batik) inspired artists in Belgium, France, Switzerland and Germany. After the First World War, batik became a popular craft in all of Europe, North America and Australia, widening the multicultural design crucible carved by Dutch involvement in trade to the East.

It is fitting that resistance to mechanised textile production took on dramatic form in the country that had suffered the most intense repercussions from mechanisation and the chemical industries: India. In the discussion about economic nationalism that emerged in India towards the end of the nineteenth century, the history of cotton production was central. It was to gain international attention through the semiotics of Mahatma Gandhi's dress. If Italy protected her economic welfare behind a black shield in response to the surge in polychrome textile products from northern Europe, the shield used by Gandhi was the white of unbleached cotton called '*khadi*'. The *swadeshi* movement, of which Gandhi became the leader, was about 'preferring the goods produced in one's own country even though they may prove to be dearer or less satisfactory than finer foreign products' (cited in Bean 1989: 363). English cloth became a symbol of English political domination and economic exploitation, while 'buying local' came to symbolise nationalism – a way of limiting the profits that England could gain from Indian consumers, and stimulating gains within the domestic clothing industry. The spinning wheel became a symbol of Gandhi's struggle. White *khadi* was Gandhi's choice. In India, white is associated with men and with widowhood (Tarlo 1996: 111). That Gandhi chose white is significant, given that India's fortune for more than a thousand years had been made on the excellence of her natural dyes. However, the synthetic dye industry does not appear to have been an enunciated focus of Gandhi's resistance.

SEEING THROUGH COLOUR

Colour is conspicuous. It is one of the most immediate flags of identity. Its desirability may be a human universal. These facts may explain, at least in part, the prominence of dyes and coloured cloth in even the earliest networks of world trade and their great economic significance.

In this essay I have contextualised two dramatic moments of colour infusion in European fashion in the history of the dye and coloured cloth trade throughout the ages: the introduction of Indian chintz or calicoes and the use of industrially produced synthetic dyes. It is clear that if fashion is only now going global, colour in fashion went global long ago. Moreover, political and economic factors in that trade have influenced local colour choices. In other words, this brief thumbnail sketch of historical forces suggests that while clothing selections are known to be a matter of taste informed by cultural meanings, orientations to centres of power have been playing an important yet insufficiently recognised role (in fashion literature and theory). As Schneider (1978: 429) argued with respect to the flip-flop in colour use between northern and southern Europe, 'Only a set of processes that includes inequalities in the balance of trade, as well as in the internal allocation of wealth and power, comes close to explaining the colour choices of the period.' There are two important implications of this insight. First, more work needs to be done on the connections between the details of fashion

CHRIS LEBEAU, Tripartite batik screen, 1905. Drents Museum, Assen
Chris Lebeau was one in a group of Dutch artists who expressed his ideas in batik.
His work represents a rejection of industrial, mass production.

expression and macro social/political shifts, including, among other approaches, the Herculean task of writing fashion history from the perspective of the production and trade in dyes. Second, if the black fashions of northern Europe in the Middle Ages were already informed by the 'global' trade in dyestuffs between China and the Mediterranean, then this poses a challenge. A definition of fashion globalisation is obliged to explain what is qualitatively different about the multicultural influences in fashion creation found in the current era. In the pages above, inspired by John Guy's insight that the extensive trade network built on the desire for Indian cloth yielded a vast crucible of reciprocal design influences, I present examples of what I refer to as multicultural spheres of design influence that were shaped by the British and the Dutch presence in Asian trade long before fashion was recognised as a global phenomenon.

Undeterred by deserts, mountains and cultural and military barriers, people throughout the ages have gone to great lengths, literally and figuratively, to acquire colour. Motivated by greed or the longing for colour, the conclusion is the same: colour is irresistible. However, when the political and economic consequences of the quest have proved to be too costly in economic or other terms, colours have been resisted. Until now that resistance has proved to have been of short duration and/or minimal appeal. Finally, the spontaneous enjoyment of colour prevails above restraint. This theme is closely linked to the question of whether fashion is uncontrollable or whether it can be steered. In the brief, historical sketch presented above, fashion – relative to colour – has been both. The wearing of black in the north was deeply culturally sanctioned. The Italian phase of wearing black was stimulated by sumptuary legislation in addition to the same cultural sanctions that had been observed in the north: religion, morality and mythology. Fashion, in this instance, was successfully steered. On the other hand, sumptuary legislation throughout Europe could not staunch the flow of multi-coloured calicoes from India in the seventeenth and eighteenth centuries (nor the flow of gold in the opposite direction). Fashion appears to have been out of control, whereas the *khadi* movement in India appears to occupy a middle place in the continuum between control and non-control (see Tarlo 1996 for insightful treatment of this theme). In indigenous society, the adoption of a wider range of synthetically produced colours appears to be synonymous with modernisation, a process that can be neither controlled nor stopped. Certainly, the factors that determine whether fashion can be steered deserve much more research.

In the examples above, even the resistance to colour, when expressed in black-and-white, seems to underscore the irresistibility of colour. The absence of colour – white and black –

may be less a colour choice than a political and/or economic choice that makes use of the conspicuousness of colour to make its point. When the Mediterranean controlled the western port of the lucrative East-West trade, access to tropical colour became an obvious sign of wealth. Given the effort and costliness of obtaining 'royal purple' from Mediterranean sea snails (twelve thousand Murex shellfish yielded 1.5 grams of dye, enough to dye one robe), saffron yellow (the stigmas of 75,000 Crocus Sativus Linneaus flowers yielded one pound of the dyestuff) and vermillion red (harvesting and preparing tiny cochineal and kermes insects), the flamboyant use of colour in Europe represented wealth indeed. Condemnation of bright colour for its association with luxury and wantonness was deeply rooted in Christian dogma. Colour resistance is packaged in a prevailing ideology of restraint, of morality over desire, the intellectual over the spontaneous urge. By as early as 785, the clergy of England had been 'ordered "not to wear the tinctured colours of India…"'. Ribeiro (1986: 33) notes that St Boniface singled out purple garments especially as leading to 'lust, unholy intercourse, indifference to reading and prayer, and the ruin of souls.' In contrast, black could be trusted as a 'true' colour, safe, restrained, sober, dependable, having integrity. Gandhi's decision to wear white was a choice as ascetic for India as black for Europe. Origin or symptom, colour has been distrusted for its flamboyance as though it were uncontrollable, unrestrained, superficial. The word *tintu*, meaning 'dyed' in Sicilian dialect, refers to corruption and evil (Schneider 1978: 422); *delun* in the ancient Spartan dialect meant both to dye and to cheat (Chenciner 2000: 37).[9]

It is hardly surprising that Hollywood, which could be characterised as a bastion of colour's conceptual qualities, would come down on the side of colour in the film, Pleasantville. More to the point, however, is that the film plays on the same opposition between black-and-white and colour. Similarly, there is a tendency to portray the moments of dramatic influx of new colour in Europe in terms of the same opposition, falsely depicting the recipients as emerging from drab times. This is especially remarkable given the extraordinary history of the procurement of dyestuffs, and given that both were periods of dramatically rising colour expectations in which improved access to colour appears to have primed the populations for welcoming yet more. It may just be hyperbole, but it says something about the cognitive value of black-and-white and polychrome colouration. More research needs to be conducted into the colours of resistance, especially of indigenous peoples to external political and economic domination, to further contextualise the instances presented in this essay.

PANTONE 13-1009 TP

PANTONE 18-1658 TP

PANTONE 17-1643 TP

PANTONE 18-1450 TP

PANTONE 18-1222 TP

ARCHAEOLOGY
The study of human history and prehistory
through the analysis of artefacts and other
physical remains

We try to understand the past by piecing together
the fragments still available to us, whether
re-creating a fabric, or reconstituting a story,
in rich warm tones.

COLOUR ASSEMBLAGE, View on Colour (vol. 29, pp. 138-139), Trend Union, 2004
This colour combination has been associated with the archaeological past.

POSTSCRIPT:
GLOBAL FASHION – MULTINATIONAL COLOUR

Colour in the current designer era is working hand in hand with fashion's self-presentation. Fashion no longer trickles up, or down, or anywhere in particular. It wafts, bubble-wrapped. Fashion has become images, fanciful illusions and allusions, conjured out of, and generating, intercultural myths and stereotypes (see Polhemus, this volume), packaged by image professionals in the marketing sector. Like the sweetmeat selected at random from the box, colour is deployed to serve the needs of the image. The names given to the colours are similarly selected to serve the image. Colour is an industrial product severed as completely from cultural norms and meanings as the ArtEZ fashion show outfits inspired by the outfits of indigenous peoples from around the world. The ensembles were abstracted, evocative, dis-encultured, referencing authenticity but staying far away from it. A Tibetan woman dressed in 'real' traditional clothing would have had no place in that scene. Her indigenous meaning-imbued processes of dye production were far from being a consideration. If a pre-industrial colour palette consisted of only a handful of deeply meaningful colours, post-industrial colour charts are arbitrary selections from literally millions of possibilities. No tint or tone is unavailable.

The move towards colour abstraction is particularly interesting with respect to the current system of colour trend forecasting. In the infinitely polychrome, industrialised world of today, the challenge to manufacturers of clothing and interiors has become which colour selection to make, not colour availability. Interestingly, where colour cards were once sufficient to specifically denote a selection, what is now selected are spheres, associations, moods, climates, time spirits. Colours are merely one of a set of constitutive elements, no longer the focus. In this way, abstract, dis-located, de-historicised, dis-enculturated colours are given associations *almost* like those from which they have been severed. Except that the associations are also ungrounded, unspecific, like a scent that hangs in the air and brings back memories that are too vague to situate. They evoke emotions and moods more than they specifically reference times and places.

The world has been spoiled by access to more colours than anybody knows how to name, let alone co-ordinate in their wardrobe. Trend-watchers and prognosis gurus hold the key to the success of clothing manufacturers. They blaze a trail through the forest of possibilities, allowing manufacturers to coordinate their colour selections in the ever-faster seasonal changeovers, whereby consumers are also able to coordinate their wardrobes — even with their cars and their home interiors. Marketing of style and image has become a more power-ful tool in sales than invention/production. Up until now the West has kept its hands on these marketing reins, while production has shifted back to Asia. A significant new dimension has been added to the original production theme that raises the question, 'has the current revolution fizzled out?' Dye factories have moved to Asia, but production is no longer key to fashion trends. Dye manufacturers, too, must dance to the rhythm of trends.

The dis-enculturation of colour is perhaps the greatest revolution in colour. National boundaries have become as meaningless in the colour industry — run by its multi-national directors, on multi-national capital, produced and sold multi-nationally — as cultural authenticity in globalised fashion. The colour industry walks hand in hand with fashion down the aisle; the two are devoted to each other, lean on each other, facilitate each other's whims and *raison d'être*.

The invention of synthetic dyes presents new challenges for expressions of resistance. In production terms, colour is no longer inseparable from a particular trade route, or from international relations. Moreover, the ubiquity of synthetic colour and Western clothing styles throughout the world has wiped out much memory of national colour emphases that once had to do with local geopolitical and ethnic circumstances. The flip-side of the same coin is the globalisation strategies of multinational dye producers. For example: 'Since the 1990s, [BASF] has relied on major production plants that enable it to manufacture on a global scale. The more that is produced in such world-scale plants, the lower the fixed costs are per ton and the greater the economies of scale that guarantee superior cost competitiveness on the world market.' (Abelshauser et al.: 2003: 615)

Modern forms of colour resistance appear to consist of a falling back on natural dyes, much like the Dutch batik artists at the beginning of the twentieth century. In Turkey, the famous DOBAG project started up by Harald Böhmer entails the return to indigenous, natural dyes 'to create self-financing village cooperatives' among the peasant rug weavers (Chenciner 2000: 275) and to re-acquaint the villagers with their cultural heritage (Anderson 1998). This project is reminiscent of Gandhi's economic nationalism, the important difference being that it concerns only a poor segment of a nation that is otherwise dependent on its highly developed industrial textiles sector.

Similarly, in India numerous natural dye projects have started up. The health and environmental issues that became immediately apparent when synthetic dyes were industrially manufactured have not yet been satisfactorily resolved. Poor nations such as India, where production has returned but where controls are insufficient, bear the brunt of these problems. This form of resistance may yet inform future developments of a less harmful mainstream industry. A UNDP-supported natural dye project states this explicitly: 'Traditional dye application methods, though eco-friendly, were cumbersome in nature. On the other hand, modern dye-application methods are rapid and easy, but polluting. Technologies should be developed which are both easy and eco-friendly.' (http://www.undp.org.in/programme/ Environment/natdye/dyejust.htm)

The practice of batik by two Yogyakarta (Indonesia) batik artists, Nia Fliam and Agus Ismoyo, is about getting back in touch with the mystical roots of Javanese culture. They believe that the survival of this ancient tradition, which is threatened in the mechanical age, depends on its practition-ers tapping back into their cultural heritage, the source of its authenticity. In this way, their work is directly opposed to the eclectic *haute couture* design by Jean Paul Gaultier incorpor-ating the African/Dutch wax print depicted above , and repre-sents perhaps the most radical expression of resistance. If the selection of a colour – and design – in modern fashion is like taking a sweetmeat from a box, the form of resistance chosen by these batik artists is about re-enculturation, giving an indigenous woman dressed in traditional clothing the seat of honour at a folklore show depicting fashion globalisation.

NIA FLIAM AND AGUS ISMOYO, Father Sky Mother Earth, 2005. Artists' collection
These two batik artists centred in Yogyakarta, Indonesia, take the core of their inspiration from Javanese
indigenous traditions that informed the production of ancient Javanese batik.

JEAN PAUL GAULTIER, collection summer 2005.
The haute couture dress incorporates Dutch-made wax print cloth inspired by Javanese batik for the African market.

NOTES

[1] I would like to thank Heather Wilson for her assistance in writing this chapter, as well as José Teunissen, Jan Brand, Minke Vos, Catelijne de Muinck, Elly Lamaker, Itie van Hout, Günther Frank. Loan Oei, Nia Fliam, Melanie Rozema, and Jan Hofstede.

[2] The third and fourth year students were directed in this undertaking in 2004 by their instructor, Melanie Rozema.

[3] Schneider's description of colours produced in England during the sixteenth century suggests that the dye palette was anything but compelling. It included a range of greys, goose-turd green, pease porridge tawny, sheep's colour, motley or iron grey and 'sad' colours (1978: 428).

[4] *Op het continent nam de weerstand tegen het gebruik van indigo soms dramatische vormen aan. Verbanning uit de stad, hoge boetes en het dreigen met het afhakken van de rechterhand komen in vele keuren voor….'* (Hofenk de Graaff 1985: 28).

[5] Europe and England had no staple commodities of lasting trade interest to India, so they had to part with their nation's gold stores.

[6] This is curious, given the consequences of the invention of chemical dyes for textile producers throughout the world. In hindsight, it is remarkable that the acquisition of synthetic dyes in a colourful textile tradition such as that of the Indians of Guatemala should have been given such scant mention in ethnographic reports.

[7] It is curious that the switch to synthetic colours receives little more than passing mention in Guatemalan textile studies. In part, this may be due to the fact that the transformation occurred so quickly, before intensive ethnographic work was being done. However, it is also true that the transformation appears to have inspired little ethnographic curiosity.

[8] Relatively little research has been conducted into the conceptual challenges represented by synthetic dyestuffs.

[9] One wonders whether such a vast conceptual gulf is to be found in the dyers' world, given that black is just as much a product of dyestuffs as any brighter colour.

REFERENCES

Abelshauser, Werner, Wolfgang von Hippel, Jeffrey Johnson and Raymond G. Stokes – GERMAN INDUSTRY AND GLOBAL ENTERPRISE – BASF: THE HISTORY OF A COMPANY. – New York: Cambridge University Press, 2003. BASF Aktiengesellschaft.

Anderson, John – MISSION TO THE EAST COAST OF SUMATRA IN 1823 – [Oxford in Asia Historical Reprints, orig. pub. Edinburgh, London, 1826]. London: Oxford University Press, 1971 [1826].

Anderson, June – RETURN TO TRADITION: THE REVITALIZATION OF TURKISH VILLAGE CARPETS – San Francisco: The California Academy of Sciences in Association with the University of Washington Press, 1998.

Bean, Susan. – 'Gandhi and *Khadi*, Fabric of Independence', in: CLOTH AND HUMAN EXPERIENCE – Annette Weiner and Jane Schneider, pp. 355-376, 1989.

Beer, John Joseph – THE EMERGENCE OF THE GERMAN DYE INDUSTRY – Urbana: University of Illinois Press, 1959.

Berlin, Brent and Paul Kay – BASIC COLOR TERMS: THEIR UNIVERSALITY AND EVOLUTION – Berkeley and Los Angeles: University of California Press, 1969.

Carlsen, Robert S. and David A. Wenger – 'The Dyes Used in Guatemalan Textiles: A Diachronic Approach', in: TEXTILE TRADITIONS OF MESOAMERICA AND THE ANDES: AN ANTHOLOGY – ed. Margot Blum Schevill, Janet Catherine Berlo, Edward B. Dwyer. New York: Garland Publishing, 1991.

Chenciner, Robert – MADDER RED: A HISTORY OF LUXURY AND TRADE: PLANT DYES AND PIGMENTS IN WORLD COMMERCE AND ART – Surrey: Curzon, 2000.

Dhamija, Jasleen – WOVEN MAGIC: THE AFFINITY BETWEEN INDIAN AND INDONESIAN TEXTILES – Jakarta: Dian Rakyat, 2002.

Donkin, R.A. – 'Spanish Red: An Ethnogeographical Study of Cochineal and the Opuntia Cactus'. TRANSACTIONS OF THE AMERICAN PHILOSOPHICAL SOCIETY – Philadelphia, 1977.

Frank, Günther – PERSONAL COMMUNICATION – Haarlem, March 2005.

Gage, John – COLOUR AND CULTURE: PRACTICE AND MEANING FROM ANTIQUITY TO ABSTRACTION – London: Thames and Hudson, 1994.

Garfield, Simon – MAUVE: HOW ONE MAN INVENTED A COLOUR THAT CHANGED THE WORLD – London: Faber and Faber, 2000.

Gilfoy, Peggy Stoltz – PATTERNS OF LIFE: WEST AFRICAN STRIP-WEAVING TRADITIONS – Washington: Smithsonian Institution Press, 1988.

Gittinger, Mattiebelle – MASTER DYERS TO THE WORLD: TECHNIQUE AND TRADE IN EARLY INDIAN DYED COTTON TEXTILES – Washington: The Textile Museum, 1982.

Guy, John – WOVEN CARGOES: INDIAN TEXTILES IN THE EAST – London: Thames and Hudson, 1998.

Hartkamp-Jonxis, Ebeltje – SITS: OOST-WEST RELATIES IN TEXTIEL – The Hague: Rijksdienst Beeldende Kunst, in cooperation with the Rijksmuseum voor Volkskunde, Het Nederlands Openluchtmuseum, Arnhem; Groninger Museum, Grongingen; Haags Gemeentemuseum, The Hague, 1987.

Heringa, Rens – 'Dye Process and Life Sequence: The Coloring of Textiles in an East Javanese Village', in: TO SPEAK WITH CLOTH: STUDIES IN INDONESIAN TEXTILES – ed. Mattiebelle Gittinger. Los Angeles: Museum of Cultural History, 1989.

Hofenk de Graaff, Judith – 'Tweeduizend jaar geschiedschrijving van wede en indigo', in: INDIGO: LEVEN IN EEN KLEUR – ed. Loan Oei. Weesp: Fibula-Van Dishoeck, pp. 23-30, 1985.

Irwin, John and P.R. Schwartz – INDO-EUROPEAN TEXTILE HISTORY – Ahmedabad: Calico Museum of Textiles, 1966.

Legêne, Susan and Berteke Waaldijk – 'Reverse images – patterns of absence', in: BATIK: DRAWN IN WAX – ed. Itie van Hout, pp.34-65, 2001 .

Maxwell, Robyn – SARI TO SARONG: FIVE HUNDRED YEARS OF INDIAN AND INDONESIAN TEXTILE EXCHANGE – Canberra: National Gallery of Australia, 2003.

– MODE – KLEREN – MODE. Exhibition catalogue – Amsterdam: Stedelijk Museum, 1980.

Newton, Stella Mary – HEALTH, ART & REASON: DRESS REFORMERS OF THE 19TH CENTURY – London: John Murray, 1974.

Nielsen, Ruth – THE HISTORY AND
DEVELOPMENT OF WAX-PRINTED TEXTILES
INTENDED FOR WEST AFRICA AND ZAÍRE –
M.A. thesis, Michigan State University, 1974.

Oei, Loan (ed.) – INDIGO: LEVEN IN EEN KLEUR –
Weesp: Fibula-Van Dishoeck, 1985.

Ribeiro, Aileen – DRESS AND MORALITY –
London: B.T. Batsford, 1986.

Rooijen, Pepin van – BATIK DESIGN –
Amsterdam: The Pepin Press, 2001.

Sandberg, Gösta – INDIGO TEXTILES:
TECHNIQUE AND HISTORY – London: A&C
Black, 1989.

Schneider, Jane – 'PEACOCKS AND PENGUINS:
THE POLITICAL ECONOMY OF EUROPEAN
CLOTH AND COLORS' – American Ethnologist 5
(3) (1978): 413-447.

Smit, W.J. – DE KAOTENDRUKKERIJ IN
NEDERLAND TOT 1813 – Ph.D. dissertation, De
Nederlandsche Handelshoogeschool,
Rotterdam, 1928.

Steiner, Christopher B. – ANOTHER IMAGE OF
AFRICA: TOWARD AN ETHNOHISTORY OF
EUROPEAN CLOTH MARKETED IN WEST
AFRICA, 1873-1960 – Ethnohistory 32 (2) (1985):
91-110.

Tarlo, Emma. – CLOTHING MATTERS: DRESS
AND IDENTITY IN INDIA – Chicago: University
of Chicago Press, 1996.

Van Hout, Itie (ed.). – BATIK: DRAWN IN WAX.
200 YEARS OF BATIK ART FROM INDONESIA IN
THE TROPENMUSEUM COLLECTION –
Amsterdam: Royal Tropical Institute, 2001.

Vollmer, J.E., E.J. Keall and E. Nagai-Berthrong –
SILK ROADS. CHINA SHIPS: AN EXHIBITION OF
EAST-WEST TRADE – Toronto: Royal Ontario
Museum, 1983.

Wilson, E. – ADORNED IN DREAMS: FASHION
AND MODERNITY – London: Virago Press, 1985.

Wronska Friend, Maria – JAVANESE BATIK FOR
EUROPEAN ARTISTS: EXPERIMENTS AT THE
KOLONIAAL LABORATORIUM IN HAARLEM – in:
Batik: Drawn in wax, ed. Itie van Hout,
Amsterdam: Royal Tropical Institute, 2001, pp.
106-123.

INTERNET SITES
www2.dystar.com/public/publications
/DS_10.pdf
www.vibrantgujarat.com/pp/am051.html
www.straw.com/sig/dyehist.html
(History of Dyes)
www.spellstone.com/indigo/herbal
/indigofera.htm
www.exportbureau.com/chemical/dyestuffs.ht
ml?manufacturer=3 infochems.com/chemdb/
com_list.asp?ltype=list&list=25326&lorder
=regi_date
greekproducts.com/greekproducts/saffron/
www.marginalrevolution.com/marginalrevolu-
tion/2004/08/royal_purple.html
www.btinternet.com/~sbishop100

FRANSJE KILLAARS

Fransje Killaars (born Maastricht, 1959) is a master in arranging textiles and thereby conveying their meaning. She makes space-filling installations consisting of compositions of brightly coloured lengths of cloth, woven bands, threads, cushions, carpets and blankets on floors and walls, according to a particular concept attuned to the space.

In 2003 she mounted the exhibition 'Stoffen Stalen Sits' (Fabrics, Samples, Chintz) in the Stedelijk Museum De Lakenhal in Leiden. The museum had invited her to make an installation with her personal selection from the museum's collection and to combine it with her own work in the same spaces.

On the basis of Sandra Niessen's research into colour, she is making a new, comparable presentation for 'Global Fashion, Local Tradition'.

EXOTICISM

A choice from the collection of Centraal Museum Utrecht

DRESS SKIRT

This dress skirt is modelled on a traditional kimono and was worn in the Netherlands around 1775. The jacket has a traditional shawl collar but the traditional flaps on the sleeves have been removed, following Dutch custom, or were omitted when the garment was made. The skirt is made of light blue silk with a pattern of peonies. It is lined with red silk and the jacket is padded.

From the collection of the Centraal Museum, inv. no. 8141.

CARACO

This caraco, a smock, was worn in the third quarter of the eighteenth century. The fabric is a chintz with a brown background and a pattern of pink, red and blue flowers. The same shade of blue is used for finishing the bosom of the caraco. A chintz smock is a typically Dutch form of clothing. In this picture the caraco is worn with a red skirt of mat silk satin and a 'fichu', or scarf.
From the collection of the Centraal Museum, inv. nos. 8922 (Caraco) and 6466 (skirt).

ROBE À ANGLAIS

This dress was manufactured in 1780 from chintz. A Robe à Anglaise can consist of an over-garment and a skirt or, as in this dress, the Watteau pleats are sewn onto the back in a narrowed form so that the dress has a closed skirt. With a Robe à la Française the Watteau pleats run without interruption from the neck down to the hem instead of from the waist.
The full form of the skirt is obtained by wearing little cushions on the hips.
From the collection of the Centraal Museum, inv. no. 8919.

DRESS

This dress was manufactured around 1810 from woollen twill with a decorative edging of wool and silk. The model of the dress was considered very classical at the beginning of the nineteenth century: a short bodice with a deep neckline and puffed sleeves with a skirt underneath covering the ankles. Classical antiquity had become popular at this time because of the excavations at Pompei and Herculaneum. These dresses were worn in combination with a cashmere shawl, or cashmere was incorporated into the dress itself as decoration, as with this one.
From the collection of the Centraal Museum, inv. no. 4478.

This shawl was made around 1830 in Europe from silk and wool. The short side of the peacock blue shawl is decorated with two rows of cashmere motifs in different formats in the colours white, soft red, green and ochre. The long side is decorated with a floral pattern. The cashmere patterns are often referred to as 'Paisley', from the Scottish factory at Paisley that produced imitation shawls. Here the shawl is worn 'à l'antique'.
From the collection of the Centraal Museum, inv. no. 12534.

VISITÉ

This visité or evening cloak was made around 1885 from wool, with woven cashmere patterns, and finished with a silk fringe. In the second half of the nineteenth century bustles were worn, which accentuated the buttocks but made it impossible to wear a coat. In order to keep warm, women turned cashmere shawls into loosely falling cloaks, which became extremely fashionable. This visité is beautifully decorated at the back, thereby emphasising the buttocks even more.

From the collection of the Centraal Museum, inv. no. 5039.

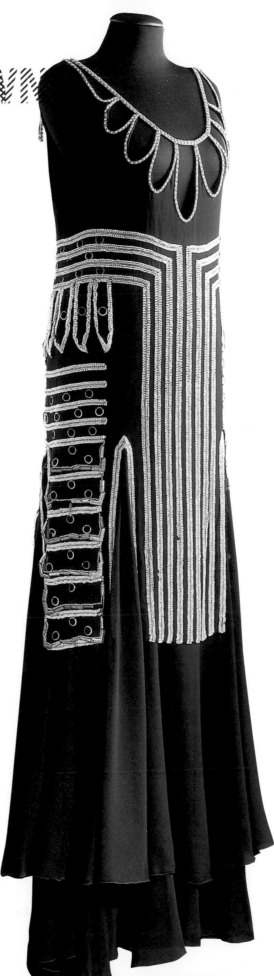

This gown was worn around 1929. Its form is typical of the twenties: straight and short, giving women an androgynous look, which was considered the acme of beauty at this period. The decoration, however, is inspired by Egypt at the time of the pharaohs. The decoration around the neck refers to the flat, round neck adornments that can be seen on the death masks and statues of the pharaohs. The decoration on the skirt is made of pearls and refers to the skirt-like forms that were worn in Egypt by both men and women.
From the collection of the Centraal Museum, inv. no. 22942.

PERSIAN CARPET BAG

This bag was made in 1970 from a Persian rug. For centuries , Persian rugs have been imparting an exotic atmosphere to our interiors. The hippies, however, thought that a Persian rug on the table was too bourgeois. The hippies were very much attracted to the exotic value of such rugs, and so they turned them into jackets or, as in this example, bags.
From the collection of the Centraal Museum, inv. no. 27199.

BATIK GARMENTS

In 1986 these indigo batik fabrics
inspired Frits Klarenbeek to make a set
of clothes for women and a set for men.
The women's set consists of a long
blouse with a raised trim and Zoave
trousers with the crotch at ankle height.
The men's set consists of a blouse, a
jacket and pleated trousers. The batik
cloth comes from Italy but is very reminiscent of Dutch wax fabrics, which we
immediately associate with Africa even
though they were produced in the
Netherlands. Attempts were made in
the Netherlands to mechanise the batik
process in order to sell the cloth in
Indonesia. The Indonesians showed no
interest, however, although the fabrics
have been hugely popular in Africa for
many years.
From the collection of the Centraal Museum,
inv. nos. 25829 (women's set) and
25830 (men's set).

BIBLIOGRAPHY

Parminder Bhachu, – DANGEROUS DESIGNS: ASIAN WOMEN FASHION AND THE DIASPORA ECONOMIES – Routledge, 2004, ISBN 0415072204.
Dangerous Designs reveals the important role played by Asian fashion in the West, both on the catwalk and on the street. The book examines the cultural codes associated with these clothes and their economic status and rejects the negative stereotyping of Asian women.

Anne Brydon and Sandra Niessen – CONSUMING FASHION: ADORNING THE TRANSNATIONAL BODY – Berg Publishers, 1995, ISBN 1859739644.
Working from an anthropological approach, the authors connect theory and practice and explain clothing habits in different periods and cultures. They do this by making connections between material culture, social and economic influences and personal taste.

Chloe Colchester – CLOTHING THE PACIFIC – Berg Publishers, 2003, ISBN 1859736661.
Describing the role played by clothing and fabrics in the history of Oceania and their influence on how the population represents its identity. Recent developments in the area of fashion and identity resulting from globalisation are also dealt with.

Diane Crane – FASHION AND ITS SOCIAL AGENDAS: CLASS, GENDER, AND IDENTITY IN CLOTHING – University of California Press, 2000, ISBN 0226117987.
Diane Crane makes a comparison between French and American society in the nineteenth century and American society in the late twentieth. She reveals a change in the message that is conveyed by means of clothes: from social class to lifestyle. She also compares the position of the nineteenth-century designer, who worked for a Parisian public with the rest of the world following suit, and the designer today who works directly for a global market.

Joanne B. Eicher, Hazel A. Litz, Sandra Lee Evenson – THE VISIBLE SELF: GLOBAL PERSPECTIVES ON DRESS, CULTURE AND SOCIETY – Fairchild Publications, 2000, ISBN 15670682.
This book presents an analysis of clothing habits, comparing Western and non-Western examples. Attention is paid not only to clothing but also to cleansing rituals and the adoration of the body. Ethno-centrism and the position of clothing habits in today's society are also dealt with.

Fredric Jameson, Masao Miyoshi – THE CULTURES OF GLOBALIZATION – Duke University Press, 1998, ISBN 0822321696.

According to an international panel of intellectuals, the process of globalisation is closely connected with the transformation taking place in economics and culture, in which the worldwide growth of consumer culture and the maintenance of national identity are important aspects. The book deals with technology, economy, sociology and anthropology. Recent global developments influence such areas as the global nature of technology, mass entertainment, communication networks and the consumer culture.

Dorinne Kondo – ABOUT FACE: PERFORMING 'RACE' IN FASHION AND THEATRE – 1997, Routledge, ISBN 0415911400.
Dorinne Kondo gives an account of her research into stereotypes of race, gender, nationality and sexuality in relation to Asia. Her conclusion is that many non-Western cultures regard themselves with an auto-exotic gaze. They look at their own culture from a Western point of view and translate this into a fashion product that they then offer back to the West.

Anoop Nayak – RACE, PLACE AND GLOBALIZATION: YOUTH CULTURES IN A CHANGING WORLD – Berg Publishers, 2003, ISBN 1859736041.
Are race, place of residence and social class still significant for today's youth cultures in a globalised world? This book shows how young people react in different ways to the recent social, economic and cultural changes that constitute today's multicultural society.

Sandra Niessen – RE-ORIENTING FASHION: THE GLOBALIZATION OF ASIAN DRESS – Berg Publishers, 2004, ISBN 1859735347.
This book deals with the ways in which the Asian fashion world is influenced by Western economics, politics and society and culture. A description is given of the resistance to the damage being done to local culture and the repercussions on modern clothing habits. The Asian fashion world is also discussed: from designers and buyers to consumers and the government.

Susan Ossman – THREE FACES OF BEAUTY: CASABLANCA, PARIS, CAIRO – Duke University Press, 2002, ISBN 082232881x.
Susan Ossman gives an account of her comparative ethnographic research into the beauty salon as a site of globalisation and cultural exchange. Notions of beauty are imitated and disseminated all over the world through the influence of magazines, films and advertising.
Alexandra Palmer and Hazel Clark – OLD CLOTHES, NEW LOOKS: SECOND-HAND FASHION – Berg Publishers, 2004, ISBN 1859738524.
Second-hand clothes are worn all over the world, but the reasons for this differ from culture to culture. This book provides a historical survey of the use of second-hand clothing and the reasons for it: economic, idealistic or simply because it happens to be fashionable.

Leslie W. Rabine – THE GLOBAL CIRCULATION OF AFRICAN FASHION – Berg Publishers, 2003, ISBN 1859735932.
African communities exist everywhere in the world, from Kenya to Los Angeles – an international network for African fashion. Leslie Rabine examines the relations and tensions that exist between the various cultures, as well as the way in which globalisation is threatening to destroy traditional techniques.

Regina A. Root – LATIN AMERICA FASHION READER – Berg Publishers, 2004, ISBN 1859738885.
Regina Root provides a survey of the influence of Latin America on international fashion. Among the topics dealt with are the importance of textiles and clothing in Latin American culture and the reasons behind it, as well as fashion icons like Frida Kahlo and Eva Perón.

Valerie Steele – FIFTY YEARS OF FASHION: NEW LOOK TO NOW – Yale University Press, 1997, ASIN 0300071329.
Valerie Steele describes developments in fashion after the Second World War, situating them in a social and cultural context. It was during this period that fashion houses switched from a local or Western platform to a global one.

Claire Wilcox – RADICAL FASHION – Harry N. Abrams, 2001, ISBN 08109658887.
This book was published in conjunction with the exhibition of the same name at the Victoria and Albert Museum in London. Three dominant international fashion trends are focused on: the invasion of Parisian houses of couture by hip British designers, the creation of highly conceptual collections by European minimalists and the almost architectural construction of contemporary Japanese clothes.

COLOPHON

This book appeared on the occasion of the exhibition GLOBAL FASHION/LOCAL TRADITION in the Centraal Museum in Utrecht from 17 September 2005 till 3 February 2006.

© 2005 UITGEVERIJ TERRA LANNOO BV
P.O. Box 614, 6800 AP Arnhem, The Netherlands
info@terralannoo.nl, www.terralannoo.nl
Terra is part of the Lannoo-groep, Belgium

First edition September 2005
Second edition January 2006

ISBN 90 5897 372 7- NUR 452

Editors: JAN BRAND EN JOSÉ TEUNISSEN

Coordination editing: CATELIJNE DE MUIJNCK

Coordination images: MINKE VOS

Text correction: NANCY FOREST-FLIER

Authors: GOSEWIJN VAN BEEK, SUSANNAH FRANKEL, SUMATI NAGRATH, SANDRA NIESSEN, TED POLHEMUS, JOSÉ TEUNISSEN, ANNE VAN DER ZWAAG

Translations: MICHAEL GIBBS

Design: CHANTAL HENDRIKSEN, Werkplaatstypografie, Arnhem, the Netherlands. Thanks to ANNIEK BRATTINGA

Printing: TRENTO, ITALIY

Text and Image exhibition: MAAIKE FEITSMA, ANNELIES SINKE

Cover:
Models: AMANDA LOPES, VANESSA GRAM
Clothes: ALEXANDRE HERCHCOVITCH
Photography: MARCIA FASOLI

centraal museum

ArtEZ Institute of the Arts

STICHTING DOEN
BANKGIRO LOTERIJ

Mondriaan Stichting
(Mondriaan Foundation)

Sikkens Foundation

Prins Bernhard Cultuurfonds geeft cultuur de kans

Fonds
Prins Claus Fonds voor Cultuur en Ontwikkeling